Contents

Biddy Baxter and Edward Barnes devised and wrote the Blue Peter Book

£2.30

Hello There!

And 1982 has been a year to remember! Prince Charles gave us a special interview about the *Mary Rose*; Sarah plunged 13 metres below the waves and passed her exams to qualify as a professional diver; Simon flew to Hollywood to photograph some ferocious four-footed film stars; Peter travelled East to report on Operation Pipeline in Java; Prince passed his puppy-walking tests; and we won three Awards!

All that, and a great deal more has happened since our 18th Book, and by the time Book number 20 is printed, we'll be celebrating the programme's Silver Jubilee – so if you've any ideas about the best way to mark twenty-five years of Blue Peter, drop us a line and let us know.

We're very proud to have been involved with two historic triumphs – the raising of the *Mary Rose* (which was why Sarah learned to dive) and Transglobe's circumnavigation of the earth by the North and South Poles.

1982 was also the year in which we successfully puppy-walked our fourth Guide Dog for the Blind. Altogether Blue Peter viewers have provided fifteen Guide Dogs, and in spite of countries like Japan experimenting with robot dogs, scientists still haven't come up with any successful substitute. To try and cope with the overwhelming demand for these animal "eyes for the blind", the Guide Dogs for the Blind Association will be opening its sixth and newest Training Centre at Middlesbrough in December.

It will be interesting to see whether Hearing Dogs for the Deaf prove to be as successful. Favour, the first-ever dog to train for this scheme in Britain, made his first public appearance on Blue Peter a few months ago, and soon there should be many more animal "ears for the deaf".

The freezing winter of 1981 took its toll of two members of the Blue Peter team. Very sadly, our tortoises, Maggie and Jim, didn't survive their hibernation – despite the efforts of expert Bob Woolley, who'd hatched them from their eggs in Leicester. We'll miss them a great deal.

When you're thirsty, no one in Britain thinks twice about having a drink of water. But for many of the people of Indonesia, the world's fifth-largest country, pure, piped water is a luxury beyond their wildest dreams. Operation Pipeline made that dream come true for a hundred and fifty villages in North and Central Java – thanks to your old stamps and coins. Peter was there when the taps were turned on at Teloguogo, and our report on page 12 records one of Blue Peter's most successful Appeals.

At the beginning of the year, we were surprised and delighted to be voted TV's best children's documentary programme by the British Academy of Film & Television Arts – or BAFTA for short. A month later, viewers of Swap Shop voted Sarah TV's Top Lady, and in May, Biddy Baxter, our Editor, was given the Pye Award for Distinguished Services to Television. If it wasn't for all your letters and ideas, Blue Peter wouldn't be possible – so these Awards are *yours,* just as much as ours – Congratulations to all our Viewers!

Simon Groom.

Sarah Greene x

Pete Duncan

Goldie

Jack

Jill

5

Giving it a whirl

"Do you fancy doing some abseiling, Sarah?"

It was Ian Oliver, known to all of us as "Olly", who is Blue Peter's Assistant Editor.

Strangely enough, I think the first time I ever came across abseiling was watching Blue Peter, long before I came on the programme. I seem to remember someone abseiling down the sheer walls of the tower block which contains the Blue Peter office, and I thought it looked rather fun.

"Yes – I'll give it a whirl," I said.

"That might be truer than you think," said Olly. "It's from a helicopter!"

All the way down in the train I kept thinking, "he's really flipped this time." How can you abseil from a helicopter? Abseiling was invented by mountaineers for descending a

cliff face by bouncing off the rock with your feet whilst you tease out the rope you're hanging from. Even I knew that. How can you bounce off thin air as you dangle from a helicopter?

"That is the problem, Miss Greene," said Petty Officer Pressley of the Royal Navy at Yeovilton where we'd come to make the film. He was tall with blue eyes, and rather stiff and formal when we first met.

"Do your friends call you Elvis?" I asked. There was a moment's pause, and then the blue eyes twinkled and the stiffness melted away.

"Yes, they do as a matter of fact," he smiled. "Well, as I was saying, we've had to find a technique that does away with the rock face."

Elvis explained that the chopper slide had been invented as a means of getting troops into an area like a

jungle, quickly, when it was impossible for a helicopter to land.

A Wessex 5 chucka-chuckened overhead and I watched with interest as Trevor Albutt, one of Elvis's colleagues, dropped like a stone from 65 metres in just 16 seconds. My interest suddenly changed to blind terror with the realisation that that was going to be me in about six hours' time!

"You're not left-handed, by any chance?" asked Marine Instructor John Smith. We were on top of a twenty-metre radio tower, and John was buckling me into an abseiling harness.

"Yes, I am." That's it, I thought. I won't have to do it because the harness won't work for left-handers. I'll go back home and nobody will think I've chickened out.

"OK," said John, and carried on buckling.

John Smith buckled me into the harness and gave me some last minute instructions

My feet were braced against the tower, but behind me was 20 metres of nothing!

The rope whirled through the figure of eight – and I dropped like a stone.

"Does it make things complicated for you – my being left-handed I mean?"

"No, not really," he said.

Silence. John's strong, efficient hands carried on buckling.

"You won't forget, will you, when I'm half-way down . . .?"

"I hope not . . . Now just put your left arm through here . . ."

I had to wear three pairs of gloves as well as the harness, but the most important item of equipment was a small metal figure-of-eight that the abseil rope passed through and around. This was the brake, and my life would, literally, hang on it.

My training was to start by abseiling down the 20-metre radio tower. This is the nearest to a sheer, unsupported drop they could find. The tower being built of metal girders had no solid wall for your feet to bounce off.

John fastened the figure-of-eight to my harness on a carabiner clip. I climbed over the rail of the tower and faced John with my back to 20 metres of nothing

"OK – you know what to do. Lift your left arm up – the rope passes through the figure-of-eight. Bring your arm down behind your back and it stops – and so do you. OK?"

I looked below and there – a tiny figure on the ground waved to me. It was Elvis. He was the brake man. If I got into trouble, one strong pull on his rope would stop me in mid-air, even if I let go altogether. With Elvis in charge, any girl would feel confident.

I braced myself against the top of the tower, took a big kick and launched myself into mid-air.

I shot down about ten metres before dropping my left arm. To my everlasting relief it worked – the rope stopped and I lurched towards the tower. I raised my arm again and heard the rope whizz through the figure-of-eight as I fell another 10 metres.

Three more times and I felt the reassuring arms of Elvis as my feet touched the ground.

"What do you reckon?" I asked.

His blue eyes twinkled again. "Brill,"

he said. And then pointed up into the air. "Back you go!"

Eight times I leapt off that tower, and eight times I climbed to the top. That's more than the equivalent of going up the 102 floors to the top of the Empire State Building without using the lift! At every descent I got slightly better, making longer and longer drops, and hitting the side of the tower less frequently. The next day, in my bath, I counted 28 blue bruises where various parts of my body had found the bolt heads and sharp corners of the Radio Tower.

Tim Hughes was the pilot of the Wessex 5, which was to take us to the dropping zone. A fine, cold drizzle began as I walked across the tarmac where the helicopter was waiting with its engines already burning.

My final fantasy: the flight abandoned for weather, and my

above the ground. My fifty kilograms was not enough to overcome the 50 metres of heavy, wet rope pulling against the brake!

going home "brave but disappointed", was quickly dispelled by John Smith who hadn't seemed to notice the rain.

We climbed in, Tim revved up the engines and we slowly rose into the bleak, darkening sky.

It all seemed so different from the quiet of the tower, John's calm voice and Elvis only a shout away.

John was only able to signal over the deafening roar of the jets, and Elvis was out of sight in the swirling rain 65 metres below.

I unfastened my safety belt and edged towards the huge open door of the Wessex. The wind almost snatched me away before I turned to make my exit.

The moment had come. I felt cold and wet and alone, but there was no going back now.

Then I began to push the rope with my left hand centimetre by centimetre through the figure-of-eight, and slowly, agonisingly slowly, I began to inch my way to the ground.

I have no idea how long it took. It felt like a lifetime. I was concentrating so much on the rope and figure-of-eight that I lost all sense of time and distance. At last, to my eternal joy, I felt Elvis's strong arms round my shoulders.

"Brill, Sarah, Brill!" he said.

I'll never use that word lightly again.

The worst moment – ten seconds before the jump . . .

I kicked off and stuck my left arm in the air – the noise of the wind and engines totally drowned the whirr of the rope through the figure-of-eight, but I felt myself fall – and then, with a sudden, sickening jerk, I stopped. I couldn't believe it. My left arm was stretched firmly above my head – and I wasn't moving. John was 10 metres above me, totally out of earshot, and I couldn't even see Elvis! I was dangling like a puppet on a string, 50 metres

. . . and the best moment – ten seconds before Elvis!

One in 1428 million!

1428 million. That's the estimated number of children in the whole of the world. And out of that colossal figure, there must be hundreds of thousands of brilliant young gymnasts, scientists, mathematicians and football players. But there's only one boy who's recorded Bach's Double Violin Concerto with the great Yehudi Menuhin. He did that when he was twelve years old – he's Jin Li and comes from Canton in China.

Every so often, a young child is discovered to have the most amazing talents. It happened over two hundred years ago when six-year-old Wolfgang Amadeus Mozart toured the cities of Europe playing his own compositions in front of Kings and Queens. And it's still happening today. In 1932, 15-year-old Yehudi Menuhin performed Elgar's Violin Concerto, conducted by Sir Edward Elgar himself.

Jin Li has been playing the violin since he was six. His parents are both musical – his mother's a pianist and his father plays the flute. Because they recognised Li had extraordinary ability, they sent him to the Shanghai Conservatory of Music when he was ten years old and since then Li has never lived at home.

When Yehudi Menuhin was visiting China he met Li and immediately offered him a place at the Yehudi Menuhin School at Stoke D'Abernon. It's one of the best music schools in the world with pupils from every Continent. But even amongst this exceptional talent, Li has emerged outstanding. Last March he played Beethoven's Violin Concerto with the London Symphony Orchestra in front of an audience of 2000 at the new Barbican Arts Centre, and his ambition is to play more and more concertos in famous concert halls the world over.

You might think a prodigy like Li would be difficult to get on with. Not a bit of it! None of us could attempt to speak a word of Chinese, but Li answered all our questions in perfect English. His eyes lit up when we talked about his football, and he made great friends with Goldie and our camera crew, who let him have a go on their cameras.

Being 5993 miles away from his family didn't seem to bother Li – there's another boy from China at the Yehudi Menuhin School, and he's made great friends with his teacher, David Takeno, who's from another Far Eastern country – Japan.

But out of all his experiences living in the West, guess what's made the biggest impact on Li? Chocolate! He'd never tasted anything like it before he came to Britain, so as a reward for playing for us, as well as his Blue Peter badge, we gave Li a giant chocolate St Nicholas.

In the years to come, when the name Jin Li may well be known as one of the greatest violin players in the world, we'll always remember the 12-year-old boy who left the Blue Peter studio with his fiddle in one hand and an enormous lump of chocolate clutched in the other!

Li's teacher, David Takeno, comes from another Far Eastern country – Japan.

Yehudi Menuhin conducted when Li played with the London Symphony Orchestra.

POT LUCK

There can't be many people who've glued a load of broken china together and ended up with a priceless Ming Jar. But that's what happened to Mr. George Cottrell when his back-yard "rubbish" was auctioned for thousands of pounds!

They say fact is stranger than fiction, and you'd be hard put to it to invent a story that sounds as far-fetched as Mr. Cottrell's Chinese puzzle. Even when I told it on Blue Peter and actually held the evidence, I found it very hard to believe.

It all began twenty years ago, in 1962, when Mr. Cottrell bought an old farm house and some land in

Oxfordshire. One day, he found a couple of dozen broken bits of coloured pot lying around in one of the yards. They'd been thrown away as rubbish, but Mr. Cottrell decided he'd try and glue them together, and although he'd never done anything like it before, he ended up with a rather nice vase.

Mrs. Cottrell thought it was lovely, even though Mr. Cottrell had patched up a missing bit on the rim with plaster of Paris, and she put it on the sideboard where it stayed for thirteen years.

And then the most amazing thing happened. One day, Mr. Cottrell was out digging his vegetable patch, which was close to the yard

These six marks prove the jar was made in the reign of the Emperor Cha Ching.

Although Mr Cottrell's £16,000 richer, he's still digging. Who knows, he might make another smashing discovery!

where the broken bits of vase had been found, when he spotted something coloured in the soil. He bent down – and picked up the missing piece from the rim! He didn't bother to put it in place, but he kept it in the bottom of the vase and didn't think much more about it until six years later.

That was when the Cottrells decided to move from the farm house into a bungalow. They decided to sell their spare furniture, but when a local antiques dealer called to give a valuation, he recognised the vase wasn't just any old pot, but a valuable Chinese jar, hundreds of years old.

When experts at Phillips were called in, they identified the jar as dating from the Ming dynasty – that's between 1522 to 1566. They could tell that from the six marks underneath that pin-pointed it as being made in the reign of the Emperor Cha Ching.

And they discovered something else. They spotted that the brightly coloured fish and lotus flowers and water weeds that decorated the jar were almost identical to another Ming jar that Phillips auctioned the previous year for a world record £220,000!

Even though Mr. Cottrell's jar had been mended, it was still extremely valuable, and when it was sold at Phillips last December, it raised £16,000.

The last clue in this remarkable Chinese puzzle is that the home of the "twin" jar that had raised the world record is a house only a short distance from Mr. Cottrell's farm. How was it that identical sixteenth century jars came to be found only a few miles apart? Were they once a pair? How did they reach Oxfordshire from China, and how were they separated? Did thieves steal one of them, hundreds of years ago, or was Mr. Cottrell's jar broken at the home of the original owner and thrown away as rubbish?

We'll never know. But for me, gardening with Percy, or on the farm at Dethick, will never be the same again. After a story like Mr Cottrell's pot luck, I'll always believe that somewhere there's another bit of Ming waiting to be unearthed.

Mr Cottrell dug up this missing piece from the rim 13 years *after* he'd discovered the rest of the broken bits of china.

The Ming jar in the photo is almost identical to Mr Cottrell's. It fetched a world record £220,000 when it was auctioned at Phillips.

What's Dirty, Wet and Dangerous?

WATER!

FACT:

Eighty per cent of all the disease in the world at any one time is caused by dirty water.

FACT:

Half the world's hospital beds are occupied by people with diseases caused by dirty water.

FACT:

These diseases cause an estimated 25 million deaths each year.

FACT:

Children are the hardest hit – in the Third World, one child in every seven dies before its fifth birthday.

Dirty Water is a Killer!

That's the first thing we discovered when a large packet of leaflets from something calling itself the World Health Organisation found its way into the Blue Peter office.

Nothing to do with the Rock group – the United Nations WHO aims to improve health and medical care in every corner of the world. The only problem is, like a lot of worthy, official organisations, the WHO isn't very good at publicising itself in a way that most people can understand. We'd certainly never heard of "The Water and Sanitation Decade 1981–1990"!

"It doesn't exactly trip off the tongue, does it?" said Sarah.

"It's been going on for a year and I never knew it existed," said Simon.

He wasn't the only one!

But in spite of such an unpromising start, the more we delved into the awful facts behind the lack of pure, fresh drinking water, the more we felt convinced we ought to try and help.

The thing that clinched it was diarrhoea.

I should think everyone in Britain's had diarrhoea some time or other in their lives. A day, or at the most two, of stomach ache and non-stop runs to the lavatory. But in the Third World, *six million* children are killed by diarrhoea each *year!*

What has gone wrong? Dirty water.

The fact is that although even the poorest person in Britain can obtain fresh water at the turn of a tap, three out of every five people in the world's poorer countries still don't have easy access to safe drinking water.

It's hard to believe that something we take totally for granted can be a luxury – but it's true!

To get an instant picture of the vastness of the problem, have a look at the North/South map. It shows very simply that one half of the world – the North – is rich, while the other half – the South – lives in dire poverty.

Some people think so what – if I'm all right, who cares about how people suffer thousands of miles away?

But in the end, if the poor countries don't survive, neither will we. The Northern countries depend on the raw materials that the Third World, as it's often called, provide – so by helping them, we're also helping ourselves. And by far the biggest need of all is for purified water. Half the people in the Third World have no clean water to drink, and three-quarters of them have no sanitation. The aim of the Water and Sanitation decade is clean water for all by 1990!

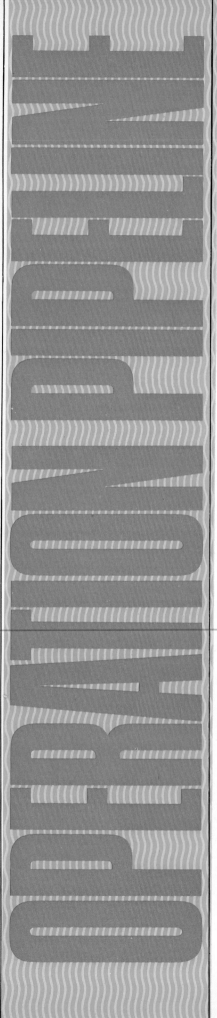

But where to begin?

What could we do and how on earth could we help? We asked our friends at Oxfam for their advice, and they told us about the schemes for pure, fresh water systems that were being planned for the Indonesian island of Java.

The problems were mind-boggling! Indonesia, the world's largest country with a population of 150 million people, consists of 13,500 islands. On Java only 12% of the population has supplies of pure water. The problem isn't that there's no rain – from November to March it's very wet indeed. Wells fill up, streams appear in the dried-up river beds and rainwater is collected from the roofs of houses. But this water is often dirty and causes many terrible diseases.

For the rest of the year, during the dry season, women and children as young as five years old, spend as many as eight hours a day journeying to and from their villages to the nearest river, carrying every drop of water they need. Each journey can be as long as two to eight miles, and the old people, and people who are ill, suffer dreadfully because they can't carry heavy loads of water.

Since 1975, schemes have been started to pipe pure water to the villages so that water is obtainable at the turn of a tap. But it's a long, hard process. The countryside is so hilly and rocky, special surveys have to be carried out for each individual village before any pipe-laying can take place. And as the villagers are so poor, it's hard for them to cover the costs of the pipes and taps – to say nothing of the costs of the surveys and the installations.

Operation Pipeline's original target was to supply piped, fresh water systems for two villages on Java. Used postage stamps were what we asked viewers to collect to pay for the pipes, and we worked out we'd need two million envelopes of stamps to reach our Target. We set up an Operation Pipeline Depot at Bicester at Oxford, and experts kept an eagle eye out for any collectors' items that viewers were generous

On Java, many women and children spend hours each day carrying heavy loads of water to their homes. Often it is dirty and causes terrible diseases.

enough to send to us for our Operation Pipeline auction at Phillips.

Two weeks later we decided we'd collect pre-decimal and foreign coins as well as the stamps, and Roadline came to our rescue with free deliveries of the coins.

The result was beyond our wildest dreams! By the end of March we'd received 5¼ million envelopes of stamps and parcels of coins – enough to provide not two, but a *hundred* villages with fresh water systems and Health Care Services.

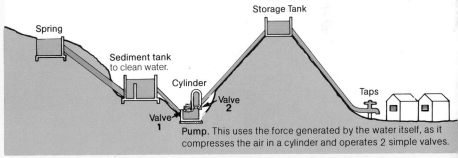

The beauty of a hydraulic ram pump is you don't need any power other than the water itself.

We demonstrated a hydraulic ram pump in the Blue Peter garden. Hydraulic ram pumps were invented about 100 years ago. They're ideal for supplying water to hilly areas and places where it's difficult to get spare parts – the only things that can wear out are the valves!

It's miraculous to think that such a basic water system can supply fresh water to 3000 or more people.

How you helped to provide clean water

What a coincidence! We discovered the grandson of the Headman of Telogoguo was living in Newcastle upon Tyne! Yanto Purwanto and his English wife, Kirsty, who is training to be a nurse, collected coins and stamps for Operation Pipeline. They hope to return to Java when Kirsty gets her SRN

Lending a hand with the stamps and coins at our Operation Pipeline Depot. You sent a colossal 5000 mail bags of stamps and 30 tons of your coins were delivered to the Depot by Roadline.

Peter's Java Report

I reported from Java for Operation Pipeline in November and March. I saw with my own eyes what the problems were, and how your stamps and coins had transformed the lives of the villages we were helping.

Larangan: An engineer shows the villagers exactly how their Operation Pipeline water system will work.

Sitiharjo: Our Health Care Services are providing scales like these to check the weight of the babies in order to spot disease early.

Larangan: Richard Holloway, Oxfam's Field Officer in Java, and I discovered the very heavy monsoon rains had washed away part of a sediment tank. The villagers made an emergency repair and Operation Pipeline is helping with proper concrete rebuilding to withstand all weather conditions!

Kaliangrek: Off to work on the pipelaying! Where water pressure is low, hollow bamboo pipes can be used as well as metal or plastic ones.

Kaliangrek: Joining up the pipes.

Telogoguo: The massive, twin hydraulic ram pumps are the largest in Java. It was a marvellous moment when I saw the fresh water with my own eyes.

Larangan: Our Health Care Services are providing sheep and goats, as well as medical supplies.

Telogoguo: These standpipes bring clean, fresh water to within a few metres of most of the villagers' front doors.

STOP PRESS!
Our Operation Pipeline Auction at Phillips broke all records for a Blue Peter Sale. Your Collectors' items raised a fantastic £47,894! Now we can help 150 villages in Java.

Prince's progress

Remember 16 March 1981? It's a date we'll never forget — when Goldie's puppies were born very early in the morning. One year later the famous five returned to celebrate their first birthday.

If you look back to page 61 of our 18th Blue Peter Book, you'll see Goldie's puppies just before they went off to their puppy walkers, and Lady began her new life on the farm at Dethick with Simon's Mum and Dad. Here's how they progressed during the next twelve months.

Prince, Henry and Buster have all completed their puppy walking so successfully, they've been accepted to go forward for their proper Guide Dog training. Sandy didn't quite make the grade and is now living as a much loved family pet in Hampshire.

We've enjoyed following Prince's progress on TV. He's the fourth dog we've puppy walked on the programme, but the very first male – Honey, Cindy and Buttons were all bitches, and it's been interesting to see first-hand how differently male pups react. For one thing they're much more boisterous and not nearly so anxious to please as bitches.

That accounts for some of the

punch-ups that have disrupted our normally calm studio atmosphere!

Strangely enough, Jack and Jill never batted an eyelid when Prince went wild. They disappeared, of course, when they'd had enough,

but the biggest fuss was made by Goldie who sometimes seemed to think she was a puppy herself when she was egged on by her son.

The whole experience of spending two days a week in a television

Learning not to react to strange noises!

A large knuckle-bone stopped Prince chewing forbidden things like shoes and furniture. This cardboard box was his first bed.

studio with all the comings and goings is excellent training for a guide dog puppy.

Guide dogs have to be friendly. They have to take their blind owners out and about on buses and into shops, so it's no good if they're snappy and bad-tempered with strange humans or animals.

In a lot of ways, the early stages of bringing up Prince were very like bringing up Goldie and at first we did the same things. Prince always enjoyed wrestling with a giant knuckle bone, which is what we gave him to stop him chewing forbidden things, like furniture or clothes, or the toys from our studio shelves.

Like all puppies, Prince was a great biter and chewer, and this had to be sternly discouraged. A Guide Dog must always be gentle, so every time we caught him chewing something that wasn't his, we'd say "No!" very firmly and give him one of his own toys to play with. His top favourite was always an old sock, padded out with rags. To our relief he learned not to bite, and he was also very quick to become housetrained.

This was doubly important – not just for Prince's future, but for the sake of our studio floor! It's painted with a white, soluble paint that dissolves when it's wet and becomes very slippery, so Prince's puddles were a dangerous hazard until he began to "ask" to go out.

After that, Prince had to get used to traffic. When he'd become accustomed to his collar and lead, I had to get him to walk on my left. Ordinary pet dogs usually walk on their owner's right, but when a Guide Dog qualifies and wears a harness, his blind owner will hold the harness with his, or her left hand, so that their right hand is free. Guide Dogs also walk just a little ahead of their owners and not to heel, like ordinary dogs. This is so that the Guide Dog can make sure the route ahead is safe.

Prince took to busy traffic like a duck to water. He's naturally curious, and I think my proudest moment came when I took him to Trafalgar Square. What with its

Prince always had a good head for heights.

I was proud when Prince walked through Trafalgar Square without chasing the pigeons.

Even Derek Freeman's budgies didn't distract Prince – a tough test for a puppy, but Guide Dogs must always be well behaved.

pigeons and fountains and tourists and the constant roar of heavy traffic, it could have been very frightening for a small pup, but Prince kept his cool. He didn't even tug on his lead as the cheeky pigeons strutted whisker-close to him. And when we walked along Whitehall to watch the Household Cavalry change the guard, his behaviour was impeccable. He was totally absorbed and fascinated by the horses and the soldiers. He didn't even make a fuss when the ceremony was over and a large crowd gathered round him.

Derek Freeman, the Guide Dogs for the Blind Puppy Walking Manager,

Out and about in London, and Prince did me proud during his test. Guide Dogs must be able to take their blind owners on tube trains.

Derek Freeman was impressed when Prince took no notice of the heavy traffic.

kept a watchful eye on Prince during the whole of his training, and last October, Prince spent five days at the Puppy Walking Centre at Tolgate for what you might call his first big test. I don't know when I've felt so nervous before – if Prince failed at this stage it would be unlikely he'd be given another chance. But as soon as I arrived at Tolgate on the day of the test, Derek put my mind at rest.

"He's been very good. He's settled well in kennels, probably better than I thought originally – I'm quite pleased with what I've seen of him so far."

That's a good start, I thought, as we set off for a walk round Leamington Spa. I crossed the road with Prince. "Let your lead go slack and walk him ahead," – Derek was testing *me* as well as Prince! But Prince was terrific – he walked very confidently right past two sets of road works with pneumatic drills juddering full-blast and turned into Leamington's biggest department store.

Prince's paws and our two pairs of feet sank into the thick-pile carpet, and even my nostrils twitched at the strong scents wafting across

from the perfume counter. We went *down* a flight of stairs and then *up* in the lift. The sliding doors and the strange clunking noises can be quite alarming for a young dog, and Derek gave him lots of reassurance. "Good boy! Mind your nose in the gates – watch your nose boy!"

After that it was out into the Parade, Leamington's busiest street. It was crowded with shoppers, but even so, Prince had to walk ahead of me without pulling on the lead. "Good boy – come back into the centre of the pavement Peter". I was concentrating too hard to wonder what passers-by were thinking as Derek gave me a stream of advice.

"Steady, steady – encourage him now, drop the lead – keep him centre – good boy!"

Last of all we went into a cake shop. Normally dogs aren't allowed inside, but Guide Dogs are an exception and Prince did me proud. He didn't even sniff at the counter, laden with doughnuts, cream buns, eclairs, sausage rolls and steak pies. My mouth was watering at the thought of a doughnut, and Derek said we could stop in the park. "Come on,

come on – keep him going, nice and fast – a slack lead."

The test was nearly over. Derek and I sat on the park bench by the river and Prince lay down. He didn't even react when I rustled the paper of the cake bag. This time it was my turn to surprise Derek.

"Happy birthday!" I said, as I handed him an iced bun.

For the first time that day, Derek looked surprised. "How did you know that? It's very good of you, Peter – thanks very much." We both sank our teeth into our buns. Prince lay still at my feet, ignoring the odd flake of icing sugar floating down towards him.

"He should know that he shouldn't," said Derek. "He shouldn't be able to relate our feeding with his feeding. He's very good you know, he's not interested at all – either in the food or the swans – and that's what a good dog should be. He's a very good puppy – and I think he's passed!"

Let's hope Prince does as well with the rest of his training, and Buster and Henry, too. This time next year, who knows, maybe all three of them will be fully qualified eyes for the blind!

P.S. Blue Peter viewers have now provided no less than 15 Guide Dogs for the Blind, and a Brood Bitch, plus buildings and equipment for every single Guide Dog for the Blind Training Centre in Britain.

The Grand Birthday Reunion!
Left to right, Goldie keeping a motherly eye on Buster, Lady, Sandy, Prince, and Henry. For proud father Danny (on the far right) Prince, Buster and Henry are the first trainee Guide Dogs he has sired.

Meanwhile back on the farm...

This year Goldie's had Lady to keep her company when I've been lending a hand on the farm at Dethick. Mother and daughter are the greatest of friends and my mum's delighted that Lady's inherited Goldie's gentle nature. If Lady ever had puppies, we'd let the Guide Dogs for the Blind Association have first pick, just as we did with Goldie's litter – it's good to think that one day Goldie's grandpuppies might be working as "Eyes for the Blind".

19

Robot Dogs

Meldog and Ar4 are dogs with a difference! But no matter how clever they are, robots can never provide the companionship of dogs like Goldie and Prince.

Meldog is an electronic Guide Dog from Japan. He's guided by landmarks in the street and can detect danger like traffic, kerbs and overhanging branches, or lamp-posts on pavements. Landmarks are stored in Meldog's electronic memory and a blind person can programme any destination into him.

Ar4, or Arthur, is the brain pooch of Steve Brooks of London. "I got the idea from *Dr Who's* K9," he told us when he brought Ar4 to the studio. But without the resources of the BBC's Special Effects Department, Steve had to use any old scrap he could lay his hands on for *his* canine robot.

That's why Ar4 has a lemon-squeezer tail, a saucepan body and back legs made from old door handles and Hoover bends.

Ar4 has radio-controlled motors for his head and his tail and the light on his collar, so taking him "walkies" is a bit like steering a tank! But all good things come to an end. "He's got so much machinery inside him, I can't fit any more," says Steve. So he's working on a giant robot spider instead!

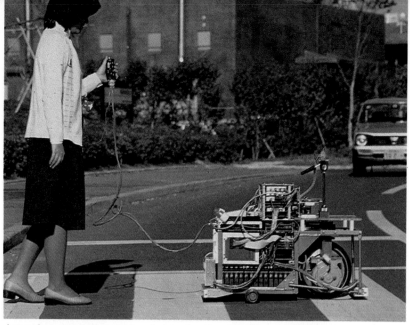

Japan's answer to canine "eyes for the blind" – a robot!

Britain's Ar4 is the creation of hospital laundry worker, Steve Brooks.

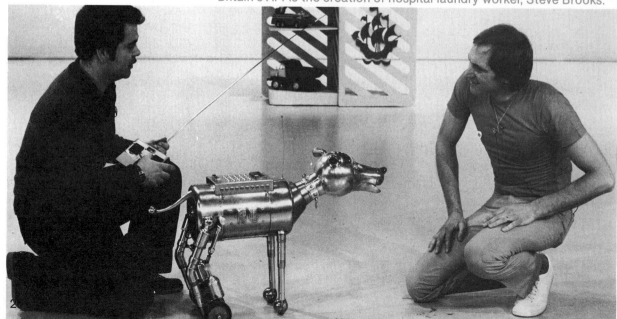

Apple Cake

Use windfall apples to make a fantastic cake that's just as good hot as cold! Add ice-cream, cream, custard, or even spread a slice with butter for an extra touch of luxury.

Ingredients

8 oz or 200 g self-raising flour.
A good pinch of salt.
4 oz or 100 g margarine.

4 oz or 100 g caster sugar.
3 oz or 75 g sultanas.
8 oz or 225 g diced apples.
2 large eggs.
Juice and grated rind of half a lemon.

Method

1   Sift the flour and salt into a mixing bowl.

2   Add the margarine and rub in lightly with the tips of your fingers. Don't over-mix as the mixture soon becomes sticky; it should look like large breadcrumbs.

3   Add the sugar, diced apples, sultanas, lemon juice and rind, and stir together with a wooden spoon.

4   Add the eggs – there's no need to beat them first – and stir until they are well mixed in. Don't beat the mixture.

5   Spoon into a 15 cm square, or 18 cm diameter round cake tin that has been greased and lined with greaseproof paper.

6   Put on to the middle shelf of a pre-heated oven, Gas Mark 4, 350°F/ 180°C and bake for 1½ hours.

On Top of the World
A Polar Triumph!

On 26 February 1979 a strange collection of packing cases and parcels was unloaded in the Blue Peter studio. They were joined by a girl with a Jack Russell terrier and four men muffled in shaggy fur jackets who sweltered under the hot lights. The British Transglobe team had reached Shepherd's Bush!

Just over three years later at 3.15 on the morning of 11 April, Ran Fiennes and Charlie Burton became the first men in the world to circle the globe the hard way – by the South and the North Poles. Bothy, their Jack Russell terrier mascot, flew from Transglobe's base camp at Alert, on the tip of Northern Canada, to join in the celebrations, and back at Television Centre, we gave a sigh of relief. Keeping in touch with Transglobe on a "live" programme via an 8000 mile radio telephone link, had had its hairy moments!

Prince Charles, Transglobe's Patron, called the expedition "gloriously and refreshingly mad". It

also demanded colossal courage and determination. From the very moment Transglobe set off from Greenwich, in London, on 2 September 1979, Ran and Charlie knew disaster would never be far away. But the intensive training that started way back in 1975 in the Cairngorms and Snowdonia, in 1976 on the Greenland Ice Cap, and continued in 1977 with the British North Pole Expedition, paid off.

As Ran and Charlie neared the last leg of the journey to the North Pole, Ginny, Ran's wife and the only girl member of the team, became the lynchpin of the Expedition, as she controlled the radio equipment at Alert, 500 miles away from the North Pole. But before that, there were innumerable hazards in the 52,000 mile journey around the world. The first triumph was reaching the South Pole in record time. Ran, Charlie and Oliver Shepherd made the fastest-ever crossing of Antarctica in the winter of 1980–81.

Then it was up the Greenwich Meridian to the roof of the world. But it was in the Arctic, with temperatures that fell to more than 50 degrees below zero that Ran and Charlie suffered their worst set-backs. They had to navigate more

than 3000 miles through the crushing ice packs of the North West Passage off Northern Canada, and then ski 300 miles to their winter base camp at Alert. Ran said his greatest fear was Polar Bears. Difficult to spot against the white wastes of the snow and ice, a charging bear can cover 45 metres in two and a half seconds. The older ones are particularly ferocious as the less able they are to hunt successfully, the more ravenous they become. Ran worked out that as a bear usually charges on all fours with its head held low, he'd aim to shoot at left-ear height, with his .44 magnum revolver strapped outside his Parka!

But the most unexpected danger came during the last 425 miles by skidoo to the North Pole, during the mildest Arctic weather on record. The melting ice made the going unbelievably treacherous. Ran nearly died when his skidoo – a snowmobile pulling a sledge, broke the ice and fell into the sea below. Charlie managed to hang on to it as

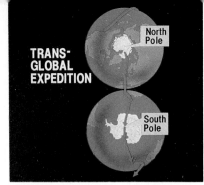

TRANS-GLOBAL EXPEDITION

North Pole

South Pole

The route for circling the world the hard way – by the South and the North Poles.

The Transglobe team in the Blue Peter studio way back in 1979 – little did we know then what adventures were in store for them.

Sleds pulled by skidoos carried the Expedition's supplies.

Ran salvaged as many of the precious supplies as he could. But there was no chance of a replacement – a fire at Alert had destroyed their spare vehicles and Ran and Charlie had to continue their icy slog on foot. After that, disasters came thick and fast. The Expedition's support plane damaged a wing in a storm, and Ran and Charlie were in serious danger when they were marooned

on a 275-metre ice flow. The whole time there was the nagging worry they *had* to reach the Pole by 15 April , the date when the ice was due to break up completely, and make the route impassable for a whole year.

But by the skin of their teeth, they made it! Thirty-one months after leaving Greenwich, a British flag flew at the North Pole. Ginny radioed the triumphant news to the outside world; Prince Charles radioed a telegram of congratulations, and Ran and Charlie cracked a bottle of whisky and a chocolate Easter egg – both dropped by plane, together with Bothy and the other members of the team for a triumphant reunion. As for Bothy – he's created a record, too. Equipped with his special Arctic survival suit, he's not only the first *dog* in the world to have been to both Poles, he's the smallest to have been to either!

Even your breath freezes at –40°C.

The *Benjamin Bowring* – Transglobe's supply ship – moored at Fimbulisen, Antarctica, with only the penguins for company.

Bothy – the first dog in the world to have been to both poles – in his arctic survival suit.

Ginny reported to us via the radio-telephone at Transglobe's base camp at Alert – 8000 miles from the Blue Peter studio.

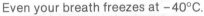

A TIGHT SQUEEZE

I'll never forget the day I took a deep breath and was laced into a corset a hundred and twenty-six years old! But I didn't suffer alone. Maggie Philbin, Isla St Clair, Tina Heath and my sister Laura, were pretty strung up, too, as we investigated the biggest collection of corsets in the world.

It seems incredible in the 1980s that underwear like this was worn within living memory. And don't think that children were let off – they weren't! Both girls *and* boys wore corsets, too. And very hot and uncomfortable it must have been.

But the interesting thing about the weird and wonderful underclothes displayed in the Blue Peter studio

last autumn is that they were all made or collected by the same firm – Symingtons.

Their business began in a small shop in Market Harborough, way back in 1830. The firm was founded by James Symington, a Tailor, Hatter and Woollen Draper. He married the teenage-girl next door – Sarah Gold – who made beautifully hand-stitched whalebone "stays" that fashionable ladies wore underneath their dresses to give them tiny waists. So James added staymaking to his tailoring business.

James and Sarah Symington had ten children and their eldest son, Robert, went to America when he was eighteen, where quite by

chance, he met Isaac Merritt Singer, the first man in the world to invent a sewing machine that gave a continuous stitch.

In 1855, Robert persuaded Singer to send one of his sewing machines to his mother in England, and Symingtons became one of the first firms ever to produce machine-made corsets.

The one I wore in the studio proved that dressing in the mid-eighteen hundreds was a lot more complicated than it is today. You couldn't possibly put on a corset on your own because of the network of laces at the back. Your maid would have to pull them up – probably with you hanging on to a bedpost for dear life, until your waist was squeezed smaller and smaller.

No wonder ladies were always having the vapours and fainting! And apart from being squeezed in, they couldn't bend either, because of the rigid support of metal or wood down the front of the corset, called a busk.

By now, the firm of Symingtons had expanded and they'd opened four other factories. It was a go-ahead firm, always on the lookout for new inventions – like using steam to mould the corsets into shape.

But by the end of the 1890s the wasp waist began to go out of fashion. A new and straighter shape was introduced, and ladies began to demand greater freedom. The Sports-woman's corset was cut low under the bust and high over the hips to give more freedom during what was called "sporting activities", like tennis, golf, hockey and cycling. Suspenders were incorporated into this design, instead of being worn separately, but the greatest freedom of all was provided by its "divided busk". The long hard strip of metal or wood down the front of the corset was now divided in two so that a lady could fasten it up without the help of a maid.

In 1911 corsets were still very complicated. Tina modelled the "New Jenyns Patent Reducing and Supporting Corset", whose secret ingredient was the interweaving of its twenty-four long laces that could be adjusted individually to give a perfect fit. And ladies were advised to put it on "in the recumbent position" – in other words, lying down – so that all their vital organs were in the right position!

The First World War brought tremendous changes in fashion. Suddenly curves were out and the straight "flapper" line was in. Then in the 1930s, new stretch fabrics were invented, using latex rubber, and the rigid lacing was replaced by stretchability! Curves came back, but in a more natural way, and Symingtons continued to produce corsets that complemented the latest fashions. And in 1939, when the Second World War broke

Some of the corsets had as many as forty narrow strips of whale bone stitched into them – but the Victorians were prepared to suffer to achieve their tiny wasp waists, and some ladies even had a couple of ribs removed so that their corsets could be pulled tighter!

Even the boxes the corsets were packed in for the shops were works of art. Today these are real Collectors' items.

The "New Jenyns Patent Reducing and Supporting Corset" was worn with a "bust improver", and the total effect gave ladies the fashionable hour-glass shape.

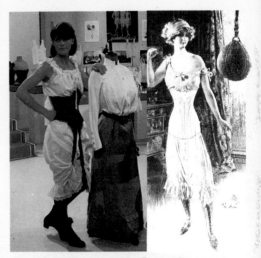

The "Sports-woman's Corset" that Isla modelled in the studio would seem a joke to Sonia Lannaman or Tracey Austin, but in 1900 it was considered extremely daring.

Hollow copper torsos had steam piped into them. The corset linings, brushed with cold, wet starch were put over them and laced up. When they dried off, they kept their shape.

out, they didn't close their factories down. Instead, they helped the War effort by providing garments for the Forces and they used the new material called "nylon" to manufacture parachutes. Altogether they made more than a million of them, and hundreds of airmen owed their lives to the skill of the Symington machinists. Throughout the war no less than 25 million yards of nylon, cotton and silk were used, together with 65 million yards of rigging.

But after the war, it was back to corsets! Symingtons had by now been one of the world's leading corset manufacturers for well over a hundred years and they continued

In 1928 the "Armmori Belt for real health and beauty" was all the rage.

until 1967 when they were taken over by the giant Courtauld company.

But luckily, Symingtons' unique collection of historic corsets has survived. It was given to Leicestershire Museum, so over one thousand five hundred stay bands, Liberty Bodices, bust improvers and corsets will be preserved for ever.

It was fun wearing the corsets for one afternoon, and we certainly gave Simon and Peter a good laugh. But give me present-day underwear any time – and that goes for Tina, Maggie, Isla – and my sister Laura, too.

The Liberty Bodice – Freedom for Boys and Girls!

The corsets that children were made to wear were called "Stay Bands" and they were full of whale bone, too. Young girls wore miniature versions of the corset ladies wore, but without the very tight waist that was so fashionable. And getting dressed was complicated for them, too. After putting on your corset bodice, you'd then add your suspenders, over them you'd put your knickers – which were called "drawers" in those days – and last of all, your petticoat, before you finally added your dress.

But in 1908 there was a breakthrough. After two years of research, Symingtons invented the "Liberty Bodice", and it was an immediate success. They were made from a knitted fabric with a special sort of cloth binding running down the front and sides and back. So they never lost their shape, no matter how often they were washed, and they had buttons for fastening your knickers and your petticoat too, if you were a girl!

After stay bands and corsets, it really must have seemed like liberty to be wearing one, and the Liberty Bodice for children was so popular, it lasted right up until 1974.

The very first liberty bodice of all was modelled by six-year-old Freda Cox, the daughter of one of Symington's directors.

WANTED
C.P. ARTISTES.
ALL LINES.
ALL GENTS TO HELP WITH THE FIT-UP.
S.A.E. AND
LOWEST TERMS

This is the kind of advertisement that used to appear regularly in the acting profession's weekly newspaper, *The Stage.* **It doesn't happen so often today because since the arrival of Bingo and Television, the old family touring fit-ups are gradually dying out. But there are one or two still around, and I'm very proud that my parents' show is still alive and well – and packing them in!**

"C.P." stands for Concert Party, and a fit-up means that the company travels with every single thing needed for the show – scenery, costumes, curtains, sometimes even the stage itself. There used to be companies who toured with a portable theatre, including dressing rooms, tip-up seats, the box office and even their own lavatories. "All gents to help with the fit-up" means that on the day the show opens, in

fact, right up to the moment you step out onto the stage looking rich, opulent and glamorous, everyone is slaving away backstage fitting up the show. There isn't a star, and no one who just does the rotten jobs like sweeping the stage. *All* gents help with the fit-up, and everyone is a star. The gents do the really heavy jobs, like building the stage, whilst the ladies work equally hard, ironing the costumes and unpacking all the

props. And a prop can be anything from a pin to an elephant.

My sister Julia and I were both born when our parents were on tour. We appeared in the show as soon as we were old enough to walk on the stage, and one of my earliest memories is helping with the fit-up.

Julia is an actress who works on television and in the London theatre. You might remember her as Tricia's elder sister, Carol Yates, in *Grange Hill.* We both visit our parents as often as we can get away from London, and I often find that I spend my first morning helping Dad to build the stage whilst Julia sorts out the costumes with Mum. It would seem very strange if we didn't, and as neither parent ever stops working, it's the only chance we have of talking to them.

27

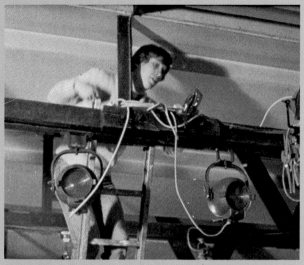

One of my earliest memories is helping with the fit-up, and when my sister and I visit the parents nowadays, we often find that I'm helping to set the lights with Dad, ... whilst Julia sorts out the costumes with Mum.

When they were doing their Old-time Music Hall in Scarborough, Dad said I could bring the Blue Peter cameras to show you what it was like, and that if I was good enough, he'd give me a part, as well as letting me help with the fit-up.

I'm shy Mary Ellen, I'm shy.
It does seem so naughty, oh my!
Kissing is nicey, I've often heard
say . . . .

"You've missed that note again," said Dad, hitting B flat insistently with his forefinger.

"Sorry!"

Kissing is nicey, I've often heard
say . . . .

"That's better, but you've got to get a bit more 'aha' into your voice."

Rehearsals were snatched between jobs like "swagging the tabs", and setting the lights, and Dad is a hard taskmaster about every detail. "Swagging the tabs", which means hanging the curtains in beautiful artistic folds, is a great theatrical craft, and my father won't tolerate tatty-looking tabs any more than he will wrong notes in a song.

Dad's energy really amazes me. When we'd more or less finished the fit-up and I was looking forward to putting my feet up with a glass of ice-cold coke, he had me out on the promenade posting bills!

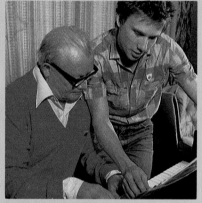

Dad was teaching me a song for the show, and much to his disgust, I kept missing a note!

Our family name is Gale, but I had to change mine to Duncan as there was already another actor called Peter Gale.

Not a moment is wasted with slave-driver Gale. All the time we were sticking playbills, he was going through our routine.

"Why can't Eve have measles in the Garden of Eden?"

"I don't know. Why can't Eve have measles in the Garden of Eden?"

"Because she's Adam!!"

"Half-an-hour, ladies and gentlemen, please!" called Julia, whilst Dad and I put the finishing touches to our make-up.

"I'm shy, Mary Ellen, I'm shy . . . ." I was praying I'd hit the right note.

My knees were trembling far more than when I did my first Blue Peter, and at that moment I would willingly have exchanged Sergeant Haynes and the underwater tunnel for my father and *I'm shy Mary Ellen. I'm shy!*

But Dad gave me a reassuring smile during the intro, and the audience all looked as though they wanted to enjoy themselves – so I licked my lips and took a deep breath . . . .

I needn't have worried. The audience knew the song far better than I did. As soon as we got to the chorus they all joined in, and when we reached *"Kissing is nicey, I've often heard tell"* – I had 200 voices to help me over that tricky note.

Dad looked really pleased.

I remembered all the gags for our front cloth patter whilst the others were getting changed for the Grand Finale, and soon the chords thundered out for *Memories* which was our closing number.

There was terrific applause from a really wonderful audience who seemed to have enjoyed every second.

I know I did – and I think Julia did, too. For us, as well as for the audience, but in a very special way, it was a moment recaptured from the Good Old Days!

"Hang on a minute, Peter, that poster's not quite straight."

"Sorry, Dad."

"What did the chicken say when its mother laid an orange?"

"I don't know. What did the chicken say when its mother laid an orange?"

Every time he gave the feed line he would look in front of him, as if talking to the audience of a packed house – and then turned at the end of the sentence so that he was looking straight at me for the punch line . . . .

"Oh, look what mama-lade!"

When we got back to the theatre it was already time to "call the half".

"Half an hour, ladies and gentlemen, please," means that in exactly half an hour you've got to be out there in front of the audience – hoping you'll remember your lines – and knowing that Dad's there waiting for that wrong note!

Dad was right beside me, sharing the same mirror as we slapped grease-paint on our faces – but even then he didn't let up.

"Why is a rock braver than a mountain?"

"I don't know, why is a rock braver than a mountain?"

"Because it is a little boulder!"

"Five minutes, ladies and gentlemen – please."

Julia was the call-boy as well as the wardrobe mistress as she helped us into our costumes for the opening number.

Dad was the old-time Music Hall chairman and sat on the side of the stage behind his desk. He called the audience to order with his gavel and announced in ringing tones:

"Ladies and gentlemen – will you welcome – Mr Peter Duncan!"

A roll of drums, a flurry of resounding chords on the piano – and I was on!

P.S. **After my film was shown on Blue Peter, Mrs. Groves, of Yorkshire, wrote to say that she and her sister were fans of my Dad when they were children.**

Dear Peter,
It was with great interest that I saw your programme featuring your visit to Scarborough to your father's Old Tyme Music Hall. I was amazed to find that your father was Alan Gale.
From 1946 – 1949 we spent our annual Summer Holiday at Redcar, North Yorkshire & were enthusiastic supporters of Alan Gale & his Wavelets

JAPAN

Land of festivals: *Two million people line the streets to celebrate Gion.*

Land of the kimono: *The traditional dress has hardly changed in one thousand years.*

Land of the Samurai: *The medieval warriors are still Japan's greatest heroes.*

A Rock 'n Roll revival – in the middle of Tokyo.

On Sunday, 5 July, I woke up late. Simon, Peter and I had arrived in Japan early Saturday evening after the 17-hour flight from London, but we'd stayed up late to try to avoid jet lag. From my room on the 35th floor of our hotel, Tokyo seemed to stretch out for ever – an endless sprawl of shining skyscrapers and tangled motorways, rooftop swimming pools, and narrow, cluttered streets. A couple of hours later, our minibus was threading its way through the densely-packed traffic and Sammy Suzuki, our driver, was calling me "Sarah-san". I had no idea what I was going to make of Japan, and our first filming stop didn't help.

We arrived at Harajuka Park to find the road sealed off. Beyond the barrier, thousands of Tokyo teenagers, dressed in black leather with "Hell's Angels" slogans or oriental dragons on their backs, were dancing to a cacophony of 1950s Rock 'n Roll music. Gangs of ten to twelve dancers were "twisting" around space-age stereo cassette players, each blaring out a song by Bill Haley or Buddy Holly. The Japanese boys all had their hair greased into a quiff, and the girls wore shocking pink skirts and bobby socks with ribbons in their hair. The Rock 'n Roll revival had hit Tokyo in a big way, and Sunday afternoon in Harajuka was the most fashionable place to be.

As we weaved our way through the dancers they looked fairly menacing in their Teddy-boy clothes, but I needn't have worried. We didn't know any Japanese, but Simon just spoke the two magic words "Elvis Presley" and their faces broke into smiles. Within seconds we were dancing to *Blue Suede Shoes*, and making our first friends of the journey.

Further into the park the clothes and music changed. Both boys and girls were wearing long flowing robes of vivid yellows, reds and greens. Their faces were exotically made up and their tapes were Japanese versions of Western disco records.

They're called "Takenoko Zoku", or "Bamboo-shoot People" because they've suddenly appeared from nowhere like bamboo-shoots after rain, but they reminded me of the Adam Ant fans I'd seen at home.

Lots of people in Japan are worried by how much young people copy Western fashions and ideas; they don't want the old ways to be forgotten. There are even special schools in Tokyo where office girls learn how to dress in a kimono, the traditional garment Japanese women have worn for centuries. I went along to one expecting it to be fairly simple, but I found out you can spend years learning the 500 ways of tying the "obi" (the sash round your waist) and perfecting the precise ritual movements for folding every length of material.

Before entering the classroom you had to take off your shoes as you do in any house in Japan, as well as in many offices and restaurants. I was given a pair of "tabi" which are a cross between white ankle socks and slippers with a separate big toe, but our film crew had to work in their socks which looked quite comical.

Up to my waist in eels, six thousand miles away from home, I decided I'd never complain again about making silage back on the farm!

Film crews get used to filming in odd places, but even Remi, our cameraman, thought twice before stepping into the water at a farm near Hamana Lagoon. I'd gone to help harvest the local crop – eels. They're considered a great culinary delicacy, and the Japanese eat 65 million of them a year. The farm had a number of large pools laid out inside enormous greenhouses. Each pool contained about 35,000 eels and I had to join Mr Tokumasu and his sons in the water where

31

they were trawling a large net. As Remi and I gingerly stepped in among the thrashing eels, he trod on one and only just saved our film camera from a watery grave. I'm used to doing some mucky, smelly jobs on my Dad's farm, but I'll never forget the stench of that eel pool, the humid heat that had me dripping before I even got in the water, the slapping sound as I emptied scoopfuls of eels into the wooden shute and the creepy feeling of eels writhing around my legs.

Oddly enough, when I finally tasted some eel Peter cooked specially for me, I liked it. What really did make me hanker for some good old fish and chips was the taste of raw squid – that I wouldn't recommend!

Sumo wrestling today is a major professional sport with a lot of money in it for the top stars. But, like most things in Japan, it has an ancient history with religious significance. Getting permission to film a training session was a problem as the only day we could manage was in the middle of a national tournament. It was like a Japanese unit asking to film England training on the morning of The World Cup! The Sadogatake stable, which trains about 60 wrestlers, finally agreed, but when we arrived at their training camp at 7 o'clock in the morning, I didn't know what to expect. The ex-Grand Champion who ran the stable was an unsmiling giant who smacked any wrestler who performed badly, with a thick bamboo stick. I changed into the heavy cotton loincloth the wrestlers wear and walked into the arena feeling like a 56 Kg weakling among the 150 Kg Goliaths. Nobody spoke English so my instructor, Kotonoryu, taught me the basic moves by a simple mime technique punctuated by grunts. It wasn't hard to follow, but I got pretty battered just learning how to fall.

I hadn't thought I'd be allowed to step into the sacred ring, but Kotonoryu suddenly beckoned me forward and I found myself in my first bout.

An actual fight is usually over in a matter of seconds. The first wrestler to step outside the ring or touch the ground with any part of his body but the soles of his feet, loses. Sure enough, in no time at all I'd been flung to the ground and I thought my chance was over. But no.

"Mo ichi-do," Kotonoryu called, meaning "One more time."

I charged him again and found myself flying through the air to hit the rock-hard clay with a thump.

"Mo ichi-do," he called again. He was granting me a great honour,

Japan's top Sumo wrestlers may not look like finely tuned athletes but the giant Kotonoryu was pretty menacing when I faced him in the ring.

but I wasn't sure how much I could take. This time I tried to lever him upwards. I got him right to the edge of the ring . . . but then he suddenly sidestepped and I ended up on my back again.

"Mo ichi-do?" he asked.

I felt exhausted, but I couldn't say no. I desperately put everything into a final charge. To my amazement it worked, and he just put a foot outside the ring. I was bruised and battered, but felt triumphant at having won at least one bout. Kotonoryu smiled and used the only English word he knew. "Champion" he said.

I thought I saw a twinkle in his eye. Had he let me win that last round? Perhaps, but I'll never know for sure.

For over 1100 years, on 17 July, the city of Kyoto, capital of Japan until 1868, has sealed off its centre for the Gion festival parade. Twenty-nine 20-metre high wooden towers are pulled through the streets in a procession which started on the decree of the Emperor in 869 to purge his nation of a great plague. Last year, two million people lined the streets and the procession was watched "live" on television throughout Japan.

A sharp-eyed TV viewer might have spotted a rather odd-looking coolie among the fifty pulling the lead float, because yours truly, Simon Groom, had been given the great honour of being invited to join the parade.

It happened when I went to meet 10-year-old Hidetaka Nakanishi who'd been selected as the "Chigo" or holy page to travel on the first float and to perform the ritual opening ceremony. I helped put the last decorations in place on the float and was offered the chance to join the parade.

Dragging the 14-ton float meant we had to work as a team.

Hidetaka wields the ritual Gion sword – with a little help from a friend!

When the day came, the temperature was 95°F. and it was hard work pulling the 14-ton float for three hours. But my ordeal was nothing compared to Hidetaka's. When I first saw him it took me a couple of moments before I realised who it was. His face was painted white, and he was dressed in ornate golden robes with a fantastic, bejewelled crown on his head. I watched, fascinated, as he raised an ancient Samurai sword above his head ready to cut a ceremonial rope and so start the parade. Then I noticed how jerky and unnatural his movements were and realised that there was a man behind him with his arms through

Hidetaka's sleeves. Nothing was to be left to chance because it would bring bad luck if the rope were not cut first time.

Thankfully all went well. The festival bells jingled and the procession moved smoothly on its way. Hidetaka had performed the ancient ritual with dignity – and with a little help from his friends!

"Momotaro Samurai" is one of the most popular series on Japanese TV. It's a bit like an oriental version of *Superman* where a masked hero always overcomes the baddies against insuperable odds. But Momotaro is a seventeenth-century warrior-knight, and his special powers lie in the brilliance of his swordplay.

I went to watch an episode being filmed on location and, although I've been in quite a few movies myself, I've never seen a film unit work faster. A 60-minute episode which would probably take three weeks to make in Britain is shot in four days by the Toei Movie Studio of Kyoto. The stories and dialogue are always much the same so there's no rehearsal and everyone is so drilled that there's never a second take, unless the star asks for one. His name was Hideki Takahashi and when I spoke to him he said he never had trouble learning his lines, only remembering the name of this week's "baddie"!

My Samurai sword fight was carefully staged by movie choreographer Mr Doi, on the set of Japans top TV series.

My sand bath was said to be good for curing hysterics.

"Mud, mud, glorious mud . . ." but the smell of sulphur was overpowering.

The series' success is due to its "tachimawari", or action sequences, when Momotaro takes on 20 villains at once and defeats them all. Mr Doi, the fight arranger, showed me how to wield a sword like Momotaro and I realised how precisely all the actors' movements had to be choreographed. The action must look breathtakingly dangerous without anyone getting hurt.

Beppu – 442 miles from Kyoto, and one of Japan's largest tourist resorts – is literally steaming! There are 3795 places alone where scalding water springs naturally from the ground. On every street corner vertical pipes belch clouds of steam into the air. The town is famous as a health resort because the Japanese like nothing better than to soak away their ills in piping hot, open-air baths. Hot-spring health hydros are everywhere, but other more exotic treatments are

Cooking eggs in Ocean Hell – they all came out hard-boiled.

available. Simon was buried up to his neck in sand which was drenched in scalding spring-water, and Peter took the plunge into a bath of hot, slimy volcanic mud!

I concentrated on touring the "Hell-pools". In many places the hot-springs are vividly coloured by minerals in the water. One is called

Blood Hell because of its dramatic red colouring, another which is a sparkling blue-green, is called Ocean Hell. Others have names like Devil's Mountain Hell, Whirlwind Hell and Golden Dragon Hell because, in the old days, it was believed they were entrances to the Underworld. I saw a Devil's Dance performed by local farmers who no longer believe in the myths, but maintain the old traditions.

We may have left Beppu with the memory of an ancient dance, but we certainly taught them a new one while we were there. One evening, the Mayor held a reception for us. The food was marvellous but at first our hosts were very stiff and formal. Then one Japanese businessman got up and sang an old folk song. We had to return the compliment, so we quickly put our heads together to see what we all knew and came up with our Blue Peter Close Harmony Group version of "*Yesterday*". The Japanese were delighted. Then they all stood up and showed us a local dance. For a moment we were all stumped – how could we respond? It was Peter who thought of the answer. For the next half-hour we taught the Mayor of Beppu and all the local dignitaries the only Japanese-sounding dance we knew – the Hokey-Cokey!

Beppu was the last stop on our expedition. In just 17 days we'd covered more than 2000 miles, visited 7 major cities and met hundreds of fascinating people. And what did I feel at the end of the journey? Exhilarated, but puzzled.

Japan is a country of contradictions. It's one of the most modern societies in the world and yet the Japanese have a greater sense of their history than any other people I've met. If you venture onto the underground in Tokyo in the rush hour you get unceremoniously pushed and shoved in every direction, and yet the Japanese have a very strict code of politeness. One of the first words I learnt from my phrase book was the Japanese word for "no" – "ie" – but I never heard it used once during the whole of our expedition!

The Honourable Pilot

Anjin Cho, a busy district in modern Tokyo, is named in memory of the first Englishman who came to Japan.

In Tokyo, my most difficult assignment was to find a place called Anjin Cho.

If you've ever got lost in a foreign town, not knowing much of the language, and not too sure of the map, you'll know how I felt.

I knew it was somewhere in the heart of Tokyo – but Tokyo is a very complicated city to get about in. They say even the postmen get lost!

I was determined to track down Anjin Cho – but very few streets have signposts, and many don't have names at all, so it was only after I'd called for advice at a local police station that I succeeded.

It turned out I was actually in Anjin Cho all the time! It means District of the Honourable Pilot, and it's called after the first Englishman who ever came to Japan.

His name was Will Adams, and his extraordinary adventures happened nearly four hundred years ago.

Will was born at Gillingham, in Kent, in 1564 – the same year as Shakespeare – near the point where the River Thames flows into the sea. When he was twelve, Will was apprenticed to a master shipwright, and from then on, ships were his life.

He learnt to build them, and to sail them and navigate, and he went on long voyages across the Atlantic to the New World.

Will Adams grew up in Gillingham in Kent which was a good place for a boy to learn seamanship . . .

. . . but he never dreamed he would end his days in Japan thousands of miles away.

Then he had the chance of a great adventure. He was asked to go as Chief Navigator with a Dutch expedition, taking five ships round the world.

Although by now he had a wife and daughter, Will Adams didn't hesitate, and he sailed on the ship *Liefde*, which is the Dutch word for Charity.

The expedition crossed the Atlantic and sailed through the Magellan Straits into the Pacific. They ran into terrible weather, with frightful storms, and at last only the *Liefde* was left, sailing alone across the vast Pacific Ocean. The twenty-four seamen left alive were so weak from illness and hunger they had to crawl across the deck on hands and knees, to sail the vessel.

Will Adams kept urging them to sail on. Then – to their enormous relief – they saw land ahead. It was the coast of Japan. Dozens of little Japanese boats came out to inspect them; they took the *Liefde*, into harbour, and the wretched seamen were carried ashore.

Will Adams was the only Englishman among the Dutch crew – so he was the first Englishman to land in Japan. The day was 19 April, 1600. The place was Kuroshima, or Block Island, and to this day a memorial stone marks the spot.

The sailors received an order, commanding their leader to appear

Shogun Ieyasu was more powerful than the Emperor of Japan himself.

Will Adams of Kent became the Shogun's respected friend.

before the Emperor's Chief Minister, the Shogun Ieyasu, and the seamen asked Will Adams to go on their behalf. They were afraid they would all be put to death as pirates.

Will Adams told the Shogun about their extraordinary voyage, and showed him his maps and charts. Ieyasu was fascinated, and ordered the *Liefde* to be sailed round the coast, so that he could see the ship for himself.

He decreed that the *Liefde*'s crew should not be put to death, but that they should not be allowed to leave Japan; they were all given rice and money, and then they split up to make a new life for themselves.

Will Adams was ordered to stay at Court. He learnt Japanese, and wore Japanese dress, and became the Shogun Ieyasu's friend and adviser.

He was asked to build a ship like the *Liefde* for Japan, and although it seemed an impossible task, he set to work with the ship's carpenter from the *Liefde* and some Japanese workmen. Between them they built a vessel of eighty tons – an Elizabethan galleon to sail in Japanese waters!

The Shogun was delighted, and Will was made a nobleman of Japan, of Samurai rank, and was given a big, country estate at Hemi – not far from Tokyo. He was a merchant and trader, a man of wealth and influence, and Will wrote: "On the twelfth of May, 1600, I came to the Great King's City, who caused me to be brought into the Court, being a wonderful costly house, gilded with gold in abundance."

He was known everywhere as Anjin Sama – the Honourable Pilot.

Only one thing was refused him. Will was not allowed to leave Japan and go back to England, so he decided to settle down and accept his fate. He married a pretty Japanese girl and they had two children called Joseph and Susanna.

Sometimes he was able to send a letter back to England by foreign

Japanese officials came on board the *Liefde* and Will Adams was ordered to go to the court of the Shogun.

merchants, and he kept urging the English to come to trade in Japan; he told them there were tremendous opportunities waiting for them.

On 12 June 1613, an English ship, *The Clove,* arrived, bringing with her the first Englishmen Will had seen for fifteen years. He took the captain to Court, and Shogun Ieyasu gave the English merchants special privileges for trading because of the high regard he had for the Honourable Pilot.

Suddenly, Will drew out from his kimono the document with the Shogun's seal that made him a Japanese nobleman. He laid it at the Shogun's feet and begged that when *The Clove* sailed back to England he might be allowed to go, too.

To his great amazement, Ieyasu agreed – and, to his even greater surprise, he realised he didn't want to go after all!

He had been away from England for fifteen years. He had become accepted in Japan, with a wife and family. Here, he was a rich and distinguished nobleman; back in England he would be only an unknown sea captain, and his family and friends would be strangers to him.

So Will decided to spend the rest of his life in Japan. For a few years everything still went well, then his fortunes changed.

Shogun Ieyasu, his friend and patron, died, and his son, Hidetada, became Chief Minister to the Emperor. Hidetada was no friend of Will's; he was jealous of his influence, and wanted to get rid of all the foreign merchants who had been allowed to come to Japan. He was afraid they would corrupt the Japanese way of life.

Will tried to help the British merchants, but he was hardly ever received at Court now, and his influence had gone.

He became ill, and at last he died, in May of 1620, when he had been in Japan for twenty years.

Shogun Ieyasu gave Will Adams a document making him a Japanese nobleman.

He wrote: "Having in my wanderings come to this land, I have, until now, lived in comfort and plenty, thanks entirely to the favour of the Shogun. Be so good as to bury me on the summit of Hemi hill, making my grave face to the East, so that I may thus behold Tokyo. My soul being in the underworld shall ever have in protection this capital city."

Within three years, all the foreign merchants were sent away from Japan. It was more than two hundred years before foreigners were allowed back in the country, and all that time Japan was cut off from the outside world.

Yet Will Adams was never quite forgotten.

The place in Tokyo I discovered with such difficulty, Anjin Cho – the Street of the Honourable Pilot – was called after him, and though Will's house has been burnt down, a little stone in an alcove marks the spot where it stood.

He was buried at Hirada, in the far west of Japan, where he died, but Will's loyal retainers erected a gravestone on his estate at Hemi, which is still there.

Even in Gillingham, his birthplace, which he never saw for more than twenty years, his name is still remembered. There is a memorial clock tower in the main street, to Will Adams, the First Englishman to set foot in Japan.

One mystery remains. What became of Will's half-Japanese children? Joseph became a pilot, and was a Christian like his father. But in 1637, as part of Shogun Hidetada's shut-down on foreign ideas, Christianity was outlawed in Japan, and many people were killed.

The last record of Joseph is that he built a Shinto shrine on the estates he had inherited from Will. And that was in 1637. Was Joseph trying to stay in favour with the Shogun, in spite of his Christian beliefs?

We cannot tell. There is no record. Joseph and Susanna may have been killed, or building the shrine may have saved them. It is nice to believe that Joseph survived and that a half-Japanese, half-English pilot named Adams lived on in Japan, into the years of isolation.

It is surely what Will Adams, English Pilot and Japanese nobleman, would have wished.

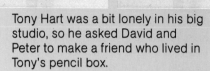

Tony Hart was a bit lonely in his big studio, so he asked David and Peter to make a friend who lived in Tony's pencil box.

Most people are amazed when I tell them that it takes a whole day to shoot a five-minute film for Blue Peter.

It was my turn to be amazed when David Sproxton told me that it takes ten days to shoot 4½ minutes of Morph. Animation is the most painstaking and the most heart-breaking process in the whole of the film world.

Twenty-five little pictures rush through the film camera in one second. Peter told me that to make Morph move, he had to expose each picture one at a time, moving Morph a fraction in between each shot. When the film is run at the normal speed, Morph moves like you see him on the television. The heart-break comes if, by mistake, you move something else in the shot which ought to remain still – like a vase on the shelf. When the film is run at its normal speed the vase will suddenly leap about and ruin the whole sequence. And you don't discover the error until the next day when the film is processed and comes back from the laboratory.

"It's not unknown," said Peter, ruefully, "to have to do a whole day's work all over again."

David Sproxton showed me how each episode begins with Patrick Dowling's script which David makes into a story board. That is a series of little drawings with the action and the dialogue written alongside each picture, together with the time allowed for the shot.

Morph is just a chunk of modelling clay, but after half an hour of pulling and pushing about in the hands of Peter Lord, he emerges as a model of a little bald-headed man with a button nose and mitten hands. But the character we all know and love as Morph doesn't come alive until he begins to move and speak. He only exists in the fantasy world of animated film – no wonder Mr Bennett doesn't believe in him!

Blue Peter viewer, Christine English, from Cambridgeshire, wrote to us saying that she was a Morph fan (with an audience of 12 million

viewers it's difficult to find someone who isn't!). Christine thought it would be a good idea if we made a film showing how Morph is brought alive.

We despatched a Blue Peter badge to Christine and I set off for Bristol to find the Morph Film Studios. This is not a vast Hollywood complex, but three rooms in a house not far from the Clifton Suspension Bridge.

Morph was created by David Sproxton and Peter Lord, and master-minded by Patrick Dowling, the Grand-Morph of the organisation who invented *Vision On* and *Take Hart*. Pat thought that

1. Peter Lord makes all the scenery and the characters, and
2. David Sproxton makes the films.

3&4 I had a go at making Morph myself.

Below: See if you can spot the one I made. The answer is upside down.

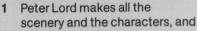
The real Morph is on the right.

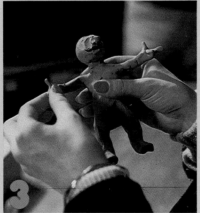

I asked David how he knew the length of the scene before he'd seen it animated.

"Peter and I act it out and time it on a stopwatch," he said.

I wondered what the neighbours thought when they looked through the windows and saw Peter and David locked in mortal combat as Chas and Morph!

Morph is so real on the screen, with such a strong personality, that I'd always thought of him as an individual – a one-off character. But Peter told me that he often makes several Morphs for one film. He tore off a piece of modelling clay and tossed it to me: "See if you can make one whilst I go and dress the set!"

After about half an hour I'd arrived at a shape that was vaguely like Morph, but entirely lacking in any character or personality. I was just about to squash it back into a ball again when Peter appeared.

"That's not bad," he said. "We might use him." Then, with a few deft strokes of his thumb, and a couple of confident lines with a match stick, the unmistakably cheeky, cocky, irrepressible character "metamorphosised". That, Peter told me, is where Morph got his name. Metamorphosis, according to the dictionary, means "a complete or remarkable change or transformation".

We were going to make a special 16-second "Morph Special" for Blue Peter in which I presented Morph with a Blue Peter badge. David and Peter had carefully "story boarded" each piece of action, taking the greatest care that Morph

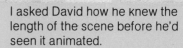

should behave in character. My part was relatively easy, although I did have to concentrate as I moved the badge towards Morph an inch at a time.

"Click" – Peter pressed a little button that exposed one frame of film.

"A little closer, Sarah – that's it." He then tilted Morph's head what seemed an infinitesimal amount. "Click" – another 25th of a second was in the can!

It took two hours of painstaking work to complete the 16-second sequence. Watching the boys' concentration on every tiny move made me realise that the real skill of the animator lay not just in making things move, but in creating a living character which is every bit as believable as a human being, but able to do fantastic and impossible things like "metamorphosising".

Peter said things like "Morph's really pleased, but he doesn't want to show it at first." And then, with an agonisingly slow series of little moves, he managed to create the atmosphere he described.

The next time you watch five minutes of Morph, spare a thought for David and Peter and the ten days hairbreadth adjustments that go towards making a piece of plasticine into a television star.

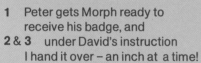

1   Peter gets Morph ready to receive his badge, and
2 & 3   under David's instruction I hand it over – an inch at a time!

Every photograph David shoots is on the air for 1/25th of a second. It took 2 hours to make this simple sequence, which in "real time" lasted 16 seconds.

> **If you want to make Morph move, trace all the small pictures and put them in order – then you can make your own flick-book.**

Are you a Finder....
or a loser?

Some people seem to have a natural talent for finding things which the other half of the world – the people with the losing streak – have unfortunately mislaid.

Two thousand years before Christ, on the Isle of Lewis in the Outer Hebrides, a farmer working by the side of a loch lost five of his best axe heads. They were carved out of stone with wooden handles, and he used them for various jobs on his farm. He must have searched high and low before giving them up as a bad job and going back to his cave to make some more.

He was a loser.

Four thousand years later, twelve-year-old Blue Peter viewer Iain MacKenzie was fishing for trout in a loch near his home on the Isle of Lewis when, through the water, he spotted some rather oddly-shaped stones. He slipped in his hand and produced five genuine stone age axe heads which were later described by top archaeologists as one of the most important discoveries of the century.

He was a finder.

Iain later made the 675-mile journey from the Isle of Lewis to the Television Centre to show his find on Blue Peter. (His home is closer to Norway than it is to London.) It was the first time he had ever been to England.

The axes are now part of the prized collection of the National Museum of Antiquities in Scotland, and Iain is the owner of a Blue Peter badge for being the most outstanding finder in the Outer Hebrides.

You can't beat Rudolph for a cheap and cheerful Christmas decoration – his sleigh can pull presents, crackers or sweets, and you can keep him to use year after year. Best of all, he's easy to make – and the secret lies with the Radio Times!

Materials

Radio Times, Cereal Packet, Tea-bag box or small shoe box, Gold gift paper or kitchen foil, Tissue paper, Black and white felt or paper, Felt (for jacket), Rubber solution glue, Sticky-tape, Flour or wallpaper paste, Matt brown paint, Red gloss paint, Gift ribbon, Tinsel, Four corks, Eight pipe cleaners, Fuse wire.

Rudolph

To Make the Reindeer

Legs, Neck and Head

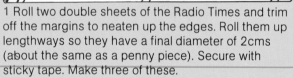

1 Roll two double sheets of the Radio Times and trim off the margins to neaten up the edges. Roll them up lengthways so they have a final diameter of 2cms (about the same as a penny piece). Secure with sticky tape. Make three of these.

Body

2 For the body do the same but use four sheets and make the diameter 4cms instead.

3 Fix two leg rolls together at one end with sticky tape.

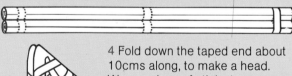

4 Fold down the taped end about 10cms along, to make a head. Wrap a piece of sticky tape around the fold to hold it in position.

5 Fold the big roll in half for the body.

6 Place the folded end half way down between the front legs and fix them with two pieces of sticky tape.

Fold remaining roll in half and fix as front legs with sticky tape.

Antlers

7 The antlers are made from four pipe cleaners twisted together for ⅓ of their length.

Two twisted together

Make two and fix them firmly with sticky tape either side of the reindeer's head.

8 Tear up several pages of the Radio Times into small pieces. Mix some flour and water (or use wallpaper paste) to make a paste to stick the pieces of paper all over the reindeer overlapping as you go.
The legs will only need one layer, but where rolls have been joined you will need more to get a smooth finish. As you work leave a long strip of paper for the tail.

Add two square pieces for the ears.

9 Then trim off the ears and make little cuts all round the edge of the tail, so it looks hairy.
When dry you can paint it using matt brown paint (either emulsion, undercoat or poster paint).

10 When the paint has dried you can add the features.
Eyes can be made from white paper with a black felt centre.
The nose is tissue paper soaked in paste then squeezed into shape and painted bright red.

11. For that extra touch you can make a jacket out of paper or felt, and hold it in place with a piece of bright gift ribbon, and you can put a shiny tinsel collar round his neck. The bells that hang on the antlers are made from scraps of kitchen foil shaped over the end of your finger and fix with a loop of fuse wire.

To Make the Sleigh

1 Sides are cut from a cereal packet (two pieces glued together are best).

Use an oblong box (shoebox or a tea bag box with the flaps cut off).

2 Cut two slits in the front of the box to take the reins.

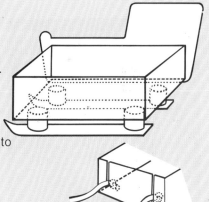

3 Paint the sleigh or cover it with gift wrapping paper.

4 For the skis, cut two strips of card and make them pointed at one end. Cover them, and four corks, with gold paper or tin foil, and bend the pointed end up slightly.

5 Then glue the corks onto the skis and stick them onto the bottom of the sleigh.

6 Use a length of gift ribbon for the reins. Tie a knot at both ends and slip the knots into the slits you cut in the front of the sleigh. Fix across the reindeer's chest, hiding the joint with a tinsel collar.

To make a smaller sleigh: if Rudolph and his sleigh are too big for your table, you can make one about a quarter of the size by making the legs with half a single sheet of the Radio Times and a whole sheet for the body. Everything else can be scaled down. Instead of corks, use pieces of pencil.

St Michael's Mount is a tiny island, rising sixty metres out of the sea. It lies three-quarters of a mile off the Cornish coast, and at high tide it is surrounded by the treacherous waters of Mount's Bay, yet at low tide you can walk out to it dry-shod.

St Michael's Mount is an island that loves to be visited. 174,000 people every year cross the causeway built five hundred years ago, and in 1981 I followed in their footsteps. Two thousand years ago, traders came here from the Mediterranean to buy the tin that lies richly in Cornish earth. In 495, fishermen saw a bright light blazing on the topmost summit of the Mount, far above the waves. They believed it was St Michael the Archangel. He stands for the fight that never ends, between good and evil, so he is always shown fighting a dragon. So now the island had a new name – St Michael's Mount. Five hundred years later, Edward the Confessor, King of England, decided to build a fine church in honour of St Michael.

Seeing

St. Michael the Archangel is the patron of both the rocky islands and all their thousands of visitors.

The elegant Blue Drawing Room was made out of the ruined monastery when St Michael's Mount became a private home.

Double

Mont St Michel lies off the coast of Normandy, in France. The dangerous tides and perilous quicksands have claimed so many victims the island used to be known as St Michel au Péril de la Mer – St Michael in peril from the sea.

King Edward knew that the other rocky island, the one off the coast of France, was dedicated to Michael as well, and already had a fine church and a monastery. So he gave St Michael's Mount in Cornwall to the Abbot of Mont St Michel in France – on condition that he founded another monastery there. All was done as the King wished – monks came and built a church. Now pilgrims visited St Michael's Mount in a steady stream, and many of them crossed the Channel to France, to visit Mont St Michel as well. They would have been surprised at their first glimpse of massive walls and strong towers, for the Mont was a strong fortress.

Mont St Michel flourished for nearly a thousand years. Then came the French Revolution, and the church and monastery were shut down. The lovely island became a prison, and the monks were the first prisoners. The buildings fell into ruins.

Across the sea, St Michael's Mount was changed utterly, too, when King Henry VIII destroyed all the monasteries in England. The Mount became the property of the Crown, and was fortified against enemies trying to invade England, like the Spanish Armada.

Both monasteries, built as places of peace to the glory of God, became monuments of war and hatred.

I'm wishing – and if I'm lucky I'll go back to the two Mounts some day. Maybe then I shall decide which one I like best!

Queen Victoria visited St Michael's Mount in 1846. It was a grand occasion with the Island's boatmen resplendent in ceremonial uniform. They rowed her across to the Mount, and a brass plate was let into the harbour where the royal foot first trod.

The Mont is surrounded by wet shimmering sand. It is said this was once all forest, drowned by tidal waves twelve hundred years ago and the Mont was a hill which became an island.

The monks took their exercise in the cloisters of La Merveille. They said their prayers as they walked past the sunny, sheltered gardens, built high up on the second floor of the West building.

Then, a hundred years ago, a wonderful change came to Mont St Michel. The historic buildings were restored, services started again in the Church, and the two-mile causeway linked the Mont to the shore. Now 375,000 tourists cross it every year to explore one of the most fascinating places in Europe. The hundred islanders are kept busy, selling food and drink and souvenirs to all their visitors!

In Cornwall, in 1659, Colonel St Aubyn, who was Captain of the Mount, was allowed to buy it for himself. It has belonged to his

The great, echoing refectory where the monks used to eat their frugal meals.

family ever since, and they live there to this day.

So the Mount, once a monastery and then a fortress, became a family home.

Today, the Mount is a whole world in miniature. Nine families live and work there. There is a tiny harbour, and boats to link them with the mainland, but often in winter the seas are too rough even for the children to go to school. The island has its own postman and fireman, and even its own fire engine, the smallest I have ever seen.

The thousands of visitors love the Mount, and many of them attend

the services held in the church on Sundays, as they have been for nine hundred years.

The church is built on a vast outcrop of rock, and the saying goes that you can put your hand on the rock and wish. I'm sure like me, that a lot of the visitors wish to come back again, because I would love to return to St Michael's Mount – and to its twin, Mont St Michel. And perhaps then I could solve the mystery – I might discover which of these fantastic, hospitable islands I like best.

Because, after one visit to each of them – I just don't know!

The bravest pilgrims climbed L'Escalier de Dentelle – the Lace Staircase – named after its delicate stone carving. They reached a gallery 120 metres above the sea, with a fabulous view.

A Gottle of Geer

Do *you* have a secret ambition? An unfulfilled dream? A feeling that one day you'll amaze your family and friends by doing something totally unexpected? I do!

Apart from my urge to be Elvis — and you can read about that on page 43 — I've always longed to be able to talk without moving my lips.

Every year, at our Party for the First Prize Winners of the competition in our Blue Peter books, we all split our sides laughing at George. George belongs to the famous escapologist, Howard Peters, and

not many people know that Howard is also an ace magician and a ventriloquist, too. Howard's ventriloquism is a bit like Tommy Cooper's magic — it all goes deliberately wrong. He's the only professional ventriloquist I know whose lips move more than his dummy's!

But joking apart, "ventriloquial art" as it's properly called, is a terrific skill and one that not many people realise has been practised for three thousand years.

When the world's first-ever book on the history and art of being a

ventriloquist was published last Christmas, we invited author Valentine Vox to the studio to give me a lesson.

Valentine started his act when he was just ten years old, and over the years he's collected two hundred dolls. Each one has its own character and its own personality, and it was a bit spooky with their two hundred pairs of eyes staring at me in the studio.

and you can read about that on page 43 —

A talking Toby jug and walking stick are two of Val's ventriloquial figures.

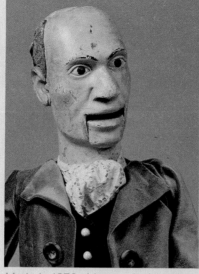

Made in 1870, this man is the oldest figure in the Vox collection.

Frank Travis, the great Victorian ventriloquist.

A tube operates granny's mouth.

I couldn't believe what I saw when I looked a bit closer. They ranged from a talking walking-stick to a talking handbag and toby-jug. Some of the heads were only a few centimetres high, although the very realistic granny sitting in a wicker chair was life-size. Her lips were controlled by pressing a rubber tube with your foot or your hand. But the oldest character in Valentine's collection was a wooden knee figure of a man, made in 1870 and used by the Victorian ventriloquist Fred Nieman. The simple spring mechanism in the jaw was controlled through the back of the head. Fred caused a stir on the stage when he operated eight figures at once, using a complicated system of wires, bulbs and tubes — as well as being all the voices. He also produced a "Ventriloquial Parliament", including the figures of three prominent politicians of the day, Mr. Gladstone, Lord Beaconsfield and Lord Randolph Churchill.

Ventriloquists were very jealous about the secrets of their figures and often patented their designs. In 1883 there was a great legal battle between the Australian ventriloquist, Frank Millis, and the Yorkshireman, Frank Travis. Millis accused Travis of stealing his crying baby idea and challenged him to a wager of £10 if he could find anything in his act that wasn't completely original.

"Practice – practice – practice!" That's Val's golden rule for mastering the ventriloquial art. The best way to make sure your lips don't move is to sit in front of a mirror.

But ventriloquism as we're used to seeing it today was started by a young man called Fred Russel in 1896. Fred pioneered the use of the single figures, which is the pattern most ventriloquists have followed ever since. His doll was a cocky cockney called Coster Joe, and together they became as famous as the Two Ronnies and Morcambe & Wise are today. Fred carried on performing until the early 1950s and was even seen on TV. Just before he died in 1957 at the age of 95, he said once when he was a boy his father had told him to keep his mouth shut. "So," he said, "I became a ventriloquist!"

That, of course, is the great art. Valentine says the most useful piece of equipment is a mirror: "Use it all the time — practise in front of it and start with the alphabet."

I did just that in the studio, and I must admit, I was far from brilliant. The "Bs" and the "Ps" were my downfall — and when Valentine asked me to have a go at "Peter Piper Picked a Peck of Pickled Pepper", the camera crew could hardly focus their cameras for laughing. If you don't believe how hard it is, try it out yourself. If you're as hopeless as I am, you can cheer yourself up with Valentine's second tip: "practice makes perfect".

"There's no special trick," he told me, "If you keep on trying, you'll get there in the end".

All I can say is that Valentine must have tried for a long, long time to reach the perfection he's attained. He can even do distant voice ventriloquism and held a phone call with an imaginary uncle to prove it.

A ventriloquist who used this technique in 1829 was arrested on a charge of kidnapping when people heard voices coming out of his suitcase! I don't think I'll ever be as good as that, but with Valentine's tips, and substituting "gs" for those difficult "ps" and "bs", I can say a "gottle of geer" with the best of them. And now I've been given my very own ventriloquial figure — Howard Peters and George may be in for a surprise at our next Blue Peter Party!

The character Charlie McCarthy became so popular in the 1930's, he starred in Hollywood films, and millions of Charlie McCarthy toys were manufactured.

In the 1950's, Archie Andrews actually had his own radio series with his "voice" – Peter Brough. Can you spot the other stars? The answers are on page 76.

You don't have to have an expensive ventriloquial figure to be a ventriloquist. An old sock or glove, like the ones we used in the studio, will do just as well.

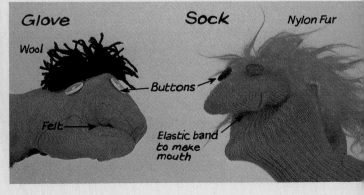

Glove
Sock
Nylon Fur
Wool
Buttons
Felt
Elastic band to make mouth

Blue Peter Film Director Alex Leger is a fairly hard guy. He served in the regular army before joining the BBC, so when he says a thing is tough, you know straight away that it's not going to be a bed of roses.

It was after I'd completed the London Marathon that he suggested that "we" – which, roughly translated, means "I" – should have a go at the Marines' Endurance course.

"Don't worry about the rain, lad, you'll be soaked to the skin in Peter's Pool .

ENDURA

Alex has a clipped way of speaking, rather like an army officer.

"Actually, it's the toughest course in any of the three services. Not everyone has survived it . . ."

"It runs across ten miles of the most beautiful countryside in Devon," he went on, as if he was selling me a fortnight's holiday.

I said, rather cautiously, that I would go and take a look at it before giving a definite answer.

The Marines at the Commando Training Centre were very nice fellows who obviously thought I was going to attempt some of the spectacular stunts without doing the gruelling 10 miles uphill and down dale slog that goes with it. They didn't exactly say so, but I got the impression that they thought I was going to bowl up in a centrally-heated caravan; bob out every so often to get mud splashes on my face, and then motor off in my well-sprung Range Rover to wait for the rest of the troop to catch up.

I must admit that after I'd seen the course, the idea was not wildly unattractive. But I don't think I could have faced a Blue Peter badge winner, a marine, or even my own reflection again if I'd given the

impression I'd done it all, when, in truth, I'd only done a half. I told them I would attempt the whole course or nothing; and then expressions changed from "he's a soft guy from television" – to "blimey, we've got a nut-case on our hands!"

It was a pleasant, if overcast day when I reported for duty to Sergeant Haynes of Hunter troop.

"I hope it's not going to rain," I said as he helped to strap the 14 kilograms of equipment on to my back.

"Don't worry about that, son, you'll be soaked to the skin when you hit Peter's Pool, anyway."

The chink of light got bigger – until I was breathing fresh air again.

He pulled the webbing strap hard across my shoulder.

"Whack it around a bit – make sure it's tight. You don't want it to move about or you'll get blisters."

"What's in it?" I asked.

"Basic stuff for survival – brushes – polish – shaving kit . . ."

I was about to say that even in London I would survive quite well without polishing my shoes or shaving, but somehow it didn't seem appropriate.

"How about your boots?" he said, looking down at my brown civilian walking boots.

"Right – fall in Hunter Troop. We're going to speed march for the first four miles. Right wheel – turn! Double march – left – right – left – right – left right – "

Speed marching is running downhill and along the flat and marching uphill (1 mile every 10 minutes) which is a very fast way to cover a long distance. The marines can keep it up for more than 30 miles at a time.

The entrance to a long black tunnel . . .

"I've brought my own because I thought they'd be more comfortable."

"You wouldn't make the first two miles in new boots, so maybe you're right," he replied.

After four miles we had ten minutes break for kit inspection before we started on the obstacle course. This, for me, was time to examine the blister on my right heel which seemed to be developing nicely. It was also a chance for Sergeant Haynes to check our water bottles. Anyone who had emptied their bottle was rewarded with a brick in their back-pack to make up the weight difference.

"Right – first three – Pickard, Jones, Duncan – on your feet. Three, two one – go!"

We were off across the heather and into the glorious Devon countryside – but not for long.

The first obstacle was a 25-metres tunnel with about 5 cm clearance on either side, and a 12 cm gap between the top of my pack and the roof. Beneath my hands and knees was 8 cm of cold, muddy water. The really frightening thing was that the tunnel zigzagged, so that after about 3 metres, I had black behind me and black in front of me. All sense of direction vanished.

"Don't panic, Duncan," I thought. "This is only the beginning!"

I crept through the freezing, stinking, black hole, and just when I was about to scream, I saw a tiny, beautiful chink of light ahead. I learned afterwards that there was a

I couldn't see the mouth of the tunnel . . . Deep breath – close your eyes – go! Jones grabbed my pack – and yanked

corporal with a spade standing on the top, ready to dig out anyone who blew their mind in the hell-hole.

Peter's Pool was next; not called after me, but after someone who hadn't made it to the other side. I didn't enquire too closely what had happened. It was a pool that started off waist deep with a sudden two-metre hole in the middle. I was quite grateful to find a rope as my pack filled with water and began to pull me under. When I came out the 14kg pack weighed

more like 30kg, but after bending over to empty out this water, it settled down to around 25kg and stayed like that for the rest of the day. I was soaked to the skin, my boots were full of water, and my blister was killing me.

"Up the hill – come on, Peter," yelled Sergeant Haynes.

Once a guy is soaking you've got to keep him moving or he'll die of pneumonia.

The next was the one where tough marines have been known to bottle out. This was also, I later discovered, where the marines were most worried about "the guy from the telly."

It was quite simply, a 3-metre tunnel. It was about 60 cm wide and filled to the roof with water. This was why we did the course in threes, one to shove through, one to pull through, and one to go through!

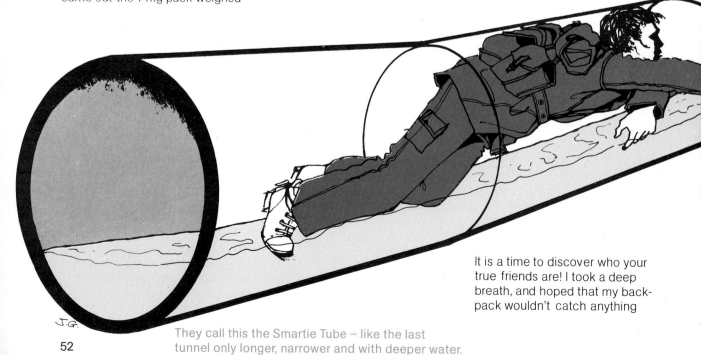

It is a time to discover who your true friends are! I took a deep breath, and hoped that my back-pack wouldn't catch anything

They call this the Smartie Tube – like the last tunnel only longer, narrower and with deeper water.

me back into the land of the living. It was better coming out than going in!

sticking down from the roof of the cave. Pickard gave me a firm shove on my bottom – and I was under. I opened my eyes for a second, but I couldn't see a thing so I closed them again quickly. I stuck my arms out in front of me and wished I was a metre taller until I felt Jones's hands close like a pair of vices round my wrists. The Beatles' hit *I wonna hold your hand* suddenly had a new meaning!

I broke the surface to hear the ever-present Sergeant Haynes:

"Come on, Peter! Run lad – run! How're your feet?"

The last tunnel was 30 metres long. It came at a time when I was physically finished, and I wondered if I had enough strength left to crawl that distance in the dark. But the thing that really got to me was that it slowly became narrower and narrower and narrower until I could only just move.

"If it gets any narrower, I'm done for!" I thought.

I saw something like a 5p piece ahead of me, which gradually became a 50p – then a tennis ball – then a football – and I was free in the light, and breathing fresh air again.

"Come on, Peter – you're doing fine! Only four miles to go!"

My blister was a sea of pain and the pack was rubbing me red raw.

"Come on – come on. Don't die on us! You've got to make it now."

I searched down to the depth of my bones to dredge up the last gram of energy.

"I'll show them I'm not a softie from the telly," I thought, and broke into a sprint.

"Are you all right?" said a voice I recognised. It was Sergeant Haynes. I had almost collapsed in his arms.

"Did I finish?" I asked him.

"Yes," he said in a voice which sounded close to amazement. "Yes – you finished all right."

Out of the Smartie Tube – only one more tunnel to go!

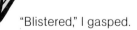

"Blistered," I gasped.

"Keep going – you can't stop now!"

Up another hill and into the Smartie Tube – far worse than the first tunnel. It was longer, narrower and with deeper water. The concrete roof kept catching on my back-pack, and worst of all, I found I was pushing a wall of water in front of me. I thought I was going to drown until I discovered the technique of wriggling along on my side like a crawl swimmer.

Nothing can be worse than that, I thought, as I ran, my heart at bursting point, up the hill. But I was wrong.

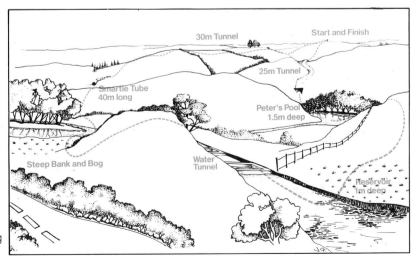

Please ask your leopard to get off my lap!

How would *you* react if someone told you you'd be sharing a bowl of cornflakes with a tiger, have a picnic with a leopard, and charge through the undergrowth standing on the back of an African elephant?

You'd more than likely say it was so far-fetched it wasn't even funny. That was my reaction one day last March when the phone rang.

"You like cats, don't you?"

It was Renny Rye, who directed our Expedition to Japan, ringing from the Blue Peter office.

"Well, I like Jack and Jill — when they're around . . ."

"They're a bit bigger than Jack and Jill," Renny interrupted — he sounded rather strange.

"Is it a Cat Show?" I asked.

"I suppose it is — in a way. Is your passport up to date?"

"Look, what's going on?"

I knew by now something must be up.

"It isn't the Blue Peter Cat Show at Olympia," said Renny. "We're going to Hollywood, and the cats are big

Buster's table manners weren't too good — but he always left a clean plate!

ones — leopards, tigers, lions, — that sort of thing."

It wasn't a dream. Hollywood producer, Noel Marshall, who'd just spent seven years making a feature film called *Roar,* had invited us to meet the stars — 115 wild animals including a rare tigon (whose father is a tiger and whose mother is a lion) and a pair of fully-grown elephants, too. After working with them for so long, he and his wife — the film star Tippi Hedren — couldn't bear to part with the animals, so they were living freely in the vast grounds of the Marshall's house where a great deal of *Roar* had been filmed.

Both Noel and Tippi have an incredible relationship with their animals. They seem totally unafraid, although they treat them with a great deal of respect and know all the warning signs that show when the lions and tigers

they work with decide *not* to be friendly. Even so, they — and all the film crew — had an amazing number of scars that proved Big Cats' claws can be sharp as knives

— even a playful pat can produce deep cuts right across a man's body. One member of the film crew had even had an ear chewed off — "Only in fun," said Tippi!

Tippi and Noel don't bat an eyelid when lions and tigers appear from nowhere.

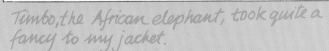
Timbo, the African elephant, took quite a fancy to my jacket.

Their enthusiasm was so infectious I quite forgot to be frightened as I was rolled over by Bugsy and Scarface, two reformed killer lions, nuzzled by Gregory, the two hundred and fifty kilo Bengal tiger, and was pushed in the lake by a lion called Brutus.

Back in Britain it all seemed like a dream. But I do have these photos and my film to prove I *did* spend two days with a leopard in my lap!

P.S. I've still got my ears, too!

Puppet on a String

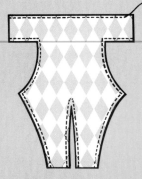

These clown puppets aren't expensive shop ones. They're all home made, and the three of them only cost about £1.50p. which is quite a bargain. If you get together with a group of friends, you could put on your own puppet panto at Christmas.

1

Fold a 30cm square of paper in half.

Mark a point 6cm from the top of the paper and draw a line 8cm in towards the fold. Call this point A.

Mark a point 15cm up the side and 3cm from the edge. Call this point B.

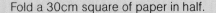

Make a mark 8cm along the bottom from the edge of the paper. Call this mark C. Draw a curved line to join A and B, and another to join B and C.

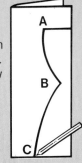

Unfold the paper. Cut carefully along all the lines you have drawn. Also make a cut 12cm up the fold. Your pattern is now finished.

Pin the pattern onto a double thickness of material. Then cut out the shape.

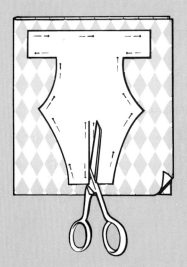

Put the two pieces of material with their right sides together. Pin round the edges, leaving the sleeve and trouser ends open.

Sew or glue the two pieces of material together along the lines of the pins. Then turn the material right side out and fold in the open sleeve and trouser ends.

To make the hands and feet, cut four blocks of wood 4cm x 2cm x 1cm.

Use sandpaper to smooth off any roughness and to round off the corners.

56

2

Use a ball of white wool for the head. (If you're short of wool, use a ball of paper for the centre and wind wool evenly over it).

Tie a bundle of strands of wool together in the centre for hair. Glue onto the top of the head.

Make the eyes from circles of felt or paper glued on top of each other.

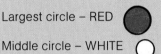

Largest circle – RED

Middle circle – WHITE

Smallest circle – BLACK

Use a red button for the nose.

The mouth can be cut from a piece of coloured felt or paper.

Glue the eyes, nose and mouth onto the head.

3

Sew the head firmly to the top of the suit.

To make a neck frill, sew a length of ribbon into a circle.

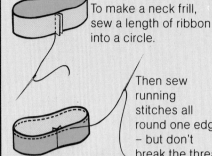

Then sew running stitches all round one edge – but don't break the thread.

Put the frill over the head and pull up the thread so that the frill fits tightly round the neck.

Finish off by oversewing a few stitches and cut off the spare thread.

Glue on small blocks of wood for ankles. Colour the shoe pieces with felt tip pen or paint.

Glue wrists and ankles and stick inside arm and leg openings.

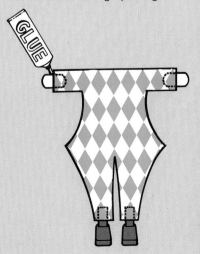

4

Make a cross piece out of 2 pieces of wood about 12cm long. Sandpaper them well and glue them together like this:

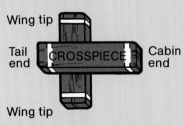

Wing tip

Tail end

CROSSPIECE

Cabin end

Wing tip

Use strong thread for the strings and attach them to the crosspiece with sticky tape. Leave them fairly long at first and adjust them so that the clown is standing in a natural position when you hold the crosspiece horizontally. When you have got this right, the strings can be glued onto the wood.

How to fix the strings

Wrist string – one length attached to each wrist and wound round tail end of crosspiece

Head string attached to end of cabin crosspiece

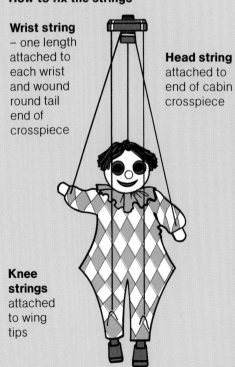

Knee strings attached to wing tips

57

A Dive through Time

It is 2.00 pm on Sunday, July 19th, 1545. The British Fleet, anchored in the Solent, is about to set sail to engage the French in battle. At their head is the *Mary Rose,* a 700 ton man-of-war, and the pride of the English Fleet. From Southsea Castle, barely a mile away, King Henry VIII watches as she puts out sail and begins to swing to starboard, her gun ports open, ready for action, the heavy guns run out, and 300 armed soldiers on station in her castles . . .

The Mary Rose sailed out of Portsmouth Harbour ready to engage the French fleet.

. . . and then, the unthinkable happens. A breeze springs up, and slowly the *Mary Rose* begins to heel over, the sea rushes in through her open gun ports, and within minutes she is sinking. The king watches with disbelieving horror as the ship, named after his sister, plunges to her death within shouting distance of the shore, and in a mere 13 metres of water.

All but thirty-five of her crew were drowned, and despite all the efforts of the King's navy to salvage her, she remained where she sank to this day. Three-quarters of the ship is encased in the mud of the Solent. That mud stopped the clocks aboard the *Mary Rose* in more ways than one. It has frozen her in time. It has preserved in perfect detail almost everything as it was on that fateful Sunday afternoon – the food the ship's cook was preparing in the galley – the fingerprints of the ship's surgeon on the ointment in his

medicine chest. It has given us, like time-travellers, a chance to go back to 2.00 pm, Sunday, 19 July 1545.

The secrets lay hidden in the Solent for nearly 300 years when in 1836 John Dean, the man who invented the diving helmet, found the wreck with his brother, Charles. They brought up some guns and ship's timbers, but after four years' work they gave up, and mud closed in once more.

I tried an officer's nit comb.

The Mary Rose Trust's Archaeological Director, Margaret Rule, showed me some of the remarkable things that have already been brought up from the wreck.

Pewter wine tankard, one of the earliest examples of English pewter. _____

Wooden serving plate _____

Gunpowder Dispenser _____

Wooden drinking jug _____

Wooden eating/serving bowl _____

Bone book spine _____

Wooden comb _____

Pomander _____

Pocket sun dial _____

I talked on the radio to diver Chris Underwood as he swam 13 metres beneath us, on station at the *Mary Rose*. Soon it would be my turn.

Margaret opened the deep freeze to reveal some of the more perishable treasures from the deep.

There it might have remained, had it not been for a local man. Alexander McKee, lives on Hayling Island about a mile along the coast from the wreck. He is an author and historian, and he learned to dive because he believed there were undiscovered and wonderful things beneath the waters of the Solent which has been the scene of so many naval battles.

In 1966, he chanced on a 19th century naval chart. In the middle of the Solent was a "X" and beneath it was written "Mary Rose".

The hunt was on, and today, hundreds of beautiful, fascinating, and incredibly preserved objects have been recovered from this time capsule beneath the waves. Margaret Rule, Archaeological Director in charge of the wreck has shown many of them to us on Blue Peter: shoes which look almost new, a pomander containing herbs to counteract the appalling smells that were obviously present below decks, a nit comb for lousy sailors! – and a beautiful ewer for serving water at the officers' table. The sight of these extraordinary things, and the enthusiasm of Margaret Rule for this journey to a lost world which

It takes 25 minutes from stepping on board to getting kitted out for a dive.

rested only 13 metres beneath the surface, made Sarah determined to go and see it for herself. That, and a memo from Prince Charles, the President of the Trust, saying he hoped that Blue Peter would take an interest in the *Mary Rose*.

But as Sarah said: "How do you get there – because it's rather a long time to hold your breath!"

My present beneath the Christmas

Tree on Blue Peter in 1981 provided the answer – flippers and a diving mask. That was just the beginning.

It didn't end there either. Every Thursday for ten weeks I went straight from the Blue Peter studio to the London Diving Centre where Reg Vallintine and Alex Doble trained me for the BSAC 3rd Class Award which I needed before I would be allowed to dive on the wreck.

In March of 1982, I dived into the murky, freezing water of Stoney Cove in Leicestershire, and penetrated the ghostly carcass of a wrecked Viscount airliner.

It was unbelievably cold, but it was fascinating to be in the cockpit of an aircraft which had once flown 3 miles high, and was now 11 metres beneath the surface of the water. I had to make 9 open sea dives to get my certificate and Margaret Rule asked me to make 3 more, in order to get experience of diving on wrecks and measuring and recording objects under the sea.

But this was all training for one goal – to make that 13 metre journey beneath the Solent, back to 2.00 pm on Sunday July 19, 1545.

I started to climb down the ladder to the year 1545

Margaret guided me through the "lentil soup" sea toward the *Mary Rose*.

It is 2.00pm on Wednesday, May 19, 1982. The weather is warm and the sea is as calm as it was on that fateful day when the *Mary Rose* put out to sea. I am on board the *Sliepner*, the supply ship of the Mary Rose Trust. Thirteen metres beneath our feet is the wreck. With me is Margaret Rule, and we are both in our diving gear about to enter the water. The moment for my dive through time has arrived.

We slip beneath the waves and slowly, hand over hand, make our way down the shot line which guides us through the murky waters to the place where the *Mary Rose* has rested for 437 years. *Prince Charles said after one of his dives that it was like swimming through lentil soup.* Margaret, who was made over 800 dives on the wreck, takes my hand and guides me towards a yellow scaffolding pole which marks one of the sections of the ship. Every section is numbered so that the divers can give reference points for everything they find. We pull ourselves along the yellow pole using flippers as little as possible so as not to disturb the silt and cloud the water even more. Suddenly we are enveloped by a huge bank of seaweed and the lentil soup turns into a swirling salad.

For a moment Margaret disappears, and then, thankfully, I see her stream of bubbles again. We turn, and gradually I can work out the shape of the timbers. There she is: the *Mary Rose*, looking for all the world as though she had sunk

yesterday. Margaret guides me across the middle of one of the scaffolding sections. There is a gun port in the side of the hull – and a cannon ball! We stop, and Margaret scoops away some silt and reveals a huge, iron ring. Then she writes on her underwater clipboard – "An Anchor". As the silt and seaweed swirl around it, I catch sight of something else. I reach out and reveal a small, oval, wooden block, about the size of my hand. I can see Margaret's eyes light up behind her mask. I had made a find!

It turned out to be a "dead eye" – one of the blocks used to hoist the sails which had caught the freak gust of wind that overturned the Mary Rose.

My dive back through time was complete.

That was Wednesday. The next day I was in the studio for Blue Peter: and on Friday, I went to Kensington Palace to show the "dead eye" to Prince Charles.

It had been quite a week!

Two days after my dive we showed my discovery to the President of the Mary Rose Trust, HRH The Prince of Wales.

The Lor

If I'd been asked when the first submarine was invented, I would probably have guessed at the First World War – along with the tank and the first fighting aircraft.

Would you believe – it was more than two hundred years ago?

This submarine was used in action by the Americans against the British in the War of Independence in 1776. It was called Bushnell's Turtle because its inventor, David Bushnell, thought it looked like two turtle shells clamped together.

The first mission was an attempt to sink *HMS Eagle,* the flagship of the British Navy, right under the nose of the entire British Fleet.

It was the night of 6 September 1776 when Sergeant Ezra Lee, the submariner, climbed aboard and opened the valves which filled the tank beneath his feet with water. Slowly, the turtle began to sink, leaving only the conning-tower above the water. Then, using his feet to drive the propeller (the first ever invented) he began to move across New York harbour to where the British Fleet lay at anchor. The warships were there to stop vital war supplies being brought to the Americans.

The submariner was able to breathe through his snorkel and plot his course by a luminous compass. His hands controlled the rudder on the stern which steered him inexorably towards the massive outline of *HMS Eagle.*

Now the dangerous manoeuvre began. By using two hand pumps

1 Snorkel for air on surface
2 Auger drill with detachable bit for fixing gunpowder keg to hull of ship
3 Vertical movement propeller (revolving oar)
4 Pistol for hand to hand combat
5 Vertical drive handle
6 Luminous depth gauge
7 Horizontal movement propeller (revolving oar)
8 Luminous compass
9 Horizontal drive foot pedals and handles
10 Tap for taking on water to aid submergence
11 Detachable lead weight for rapid surfacing in emergencies
12 Hand pumps for taking on water to submerge
13 Winch for retrieving lead weight
14 Rudder steerage controls
15 Waterproofed gunpowder keg (150lb of gunpowder)
16 Porthole for surface vision

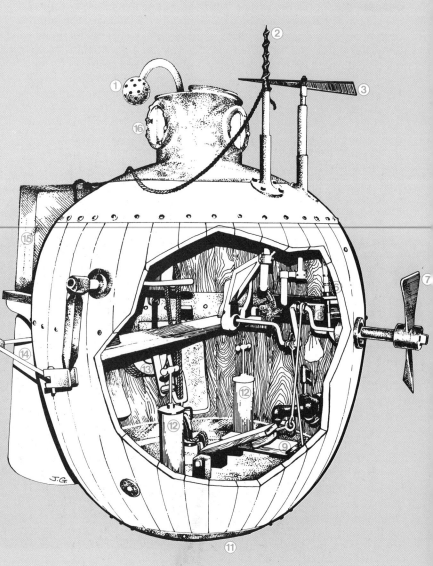

he Diver

he completely submerged his craft, and then used a propeller to get him down beneath the hull of the great ship.

He had just half an hour's worth of air in which to complete the operation.

Slowly, silently, he descended until he was directly underneath the *Eagle*.

Using a brace with a detachable bit, he began to bore a hole in the ship's bottom. When he felt the bit bite securely into the timbers, he pulled a bolt which let it go. The bit was attached to a piece of rope trailing behind the submarine. On the end of the rope was a water-proof bag containing one hundred and fifty pounds of gunpowder.

It was enough to blow the *Eagle* out of the water.

In the gunpowder case was a clockwork device which would give the pilot thirty minutes to get away before the explosion.

By now most of his air was gone. He pedalled frantically to clear the bottom of the warship, then he released the winch which dropped a two-hundred-pound lead weight off the bottom of the submarine and floated to the surface.

After a deep gulp of night air, he pedalled off to a safe distance and started the countdown for *HMS Eagle* to blast out New York Harbour.

It never happened.

The mission had been a complete success, but for one thing. The gunpowder case did not attach properly to the bottom of HMS *Eagle* and it floated off to explode harmlessly out to sea.

But the principle was proved. And the British were so frightened of another attack that they moved their ships further offshore where they were less effective in blockades the Americans supplied. The submarine, the most effective and perhaps the most evil instrument of marine warfare, had been invented.

ELVIS ELVIS ELVIS ELVIS ELVIS ELVIS

Have you ever dreamed you were someone else so clearly that for a moment you actually felt you were that person? Once you close the bedroom door you can be Keegan scoring a goal, Botham hitting for six – or even Peter Duncan completing the Marines' Endurance course! My chance came on 19 October last year when, for two glorious hours, with a lot of help from The BBC's Costume and Make-up Departments, I WAS Elvis Presley.

What's Cooking?

The Café Royal, right in the heart of London, was once a place more famous for its diners than its dinners. At the end of the last century it was the nightly haunt of all the famous writers, artistes and actors in London. They came to talk and to be seen – and above all, to be heard.

They say that Marie Lloyd, the famous Music Hall singer of saucy songs, once chased the Head Waiter round the restaurant with an 20cm hat pin – because her soup was cold.

"There is only one thing in the world worse than being talked about, and that's not being talked about!" said the great Oscar Wilde, whose sayings became as famous as his plays.

"I have nothing to declare but my genius," he once told a customs official.

His opinion of hunting was "the unspeakable in full pursuit of the uneatable."

I went to the Café Royal to pursue the eatable, but I made my entrance not through the gilded front door in Regent Street, but through the somewhat seedier back door in Glasshouse Street, over which is written: *Café Royal – Staff Only*.

The Café Royal's reputation for wit may have dimmed in the last hundred years, but its consumption of food is enormous.

"140 in number – 6 oz portions of chicken – two saddle of English lamb – 30 lb diced chuck steak." This was Executive Chef, Roger Bamfield, on the phone to his butcher. "100 lb of pork chipolatas – 20 lb of rindless back bacon – "

He broke off for a second to give me a smile and wave me to a chair. "Six in number English strip loins, two in number Parma hams – 50 lb of pork sausage."

Oscar Wilde, the great Victorian playwright whose sayings were as famous as his plays, and Marie Lloyd, the famous singer of saucy songs, used to dine regularly at the Café Royal.

This was not for a month, nor for a week, but for one day's champing of a thousand jaws at the Café Royal.

The restaurant was empty, the tables bare and dingy without their fine linen. The chandeliers were out and two young waiters in tee-shirts and jeans were emptying last night's ashtrays by the light of a single, naked bulb.

But the kitchens were a roar of activity. Steam and the crash and clatter of a hundred saucepans filled the air as Roger set me to work in my newly-starched, crisp white chef's outfit. I looked the part, if nothing else.

"Right, Simon – you're on spinach – just take the stalks out and fill up that colander."

That didn't seem too difficult – except that the colander was the size of a lily-pond, and the spinach with its stalks filled four enormous boxes.

The noise was beyond belief; and as more ovens were lit and the gigantic pans began to bubble, it became hotter by the minute.

Greek, Italian and Chinese voices yelled above the roar of the gas jets, the endless clatter of razor-sharp knives on metal, and the insistent dull crunch of the meat cleavers as they dismembered whole beasts.

An old waiter with a face like a knawed bone, loomed out of the steam.

"Les épinards viennent aujourd'hui – ou demain?" he asked, looking scornfully at my pathetic pile of spinach at the bottom of that insatiable colander. Although the waiters, chefs and kitchen porters from all over the world might speak to each other in any language under the sun, all the orders are given in French, which is the international language of food.

I looked blankly back at the waiter, and my Italian mate said:
"He wantsa to know how longa for the spinach?"

"Oh – er – deux minutes?" I said, hopefully. But thankfully, Roger appeared with reinforcements whose deft hands ripped out the stalks of the rest of the spinach in no time.

But my shame was not over yet. Duchess Potatoes – or Pommes de terre Duchesse – are beautiful swirls of potato that look as if they've been chiselled out of wood. Roger showed me how to make them by forcing mashed potatoes

Philip Beh, a Chinese Chef, carved a masterpiece out of a block of ice.

Forcing mashed potatoes through a bag to make Pommes de terre Duchesse was trickier than it looks.

I challenged Roger Bamfield to a cucumber-slicing race and lost by five minutes, two cucumbers and 2000 slices!

through a bag, like cream. The only trouble is that mashed potatoes are a lot more reluctant, and you really have to squeeze with all your might to get them out of the bag.

But if you want to look really ham-fisted, you should challenge Roger

to a cucumber-slicing race. I honestly thought I was quite good at it because I often help to prepare salads at nome. I reckon I can keep up 150 slices a minute for quite a long time. My knife strokes had the steady rhythm of a metronome, whilst Roger's blade sounded like a sustained burst from a machine gun as the wafer-thin slices flew off his knife like a green snowstorm.

In a quiet corner, Philip Beh – a Chinese chef – was making a real

snow-storm — or more correctly, an ice-storm. He was hacking away at a huge block of ice, with some really lethal-looking tools. Slowly, out of the ice there appeared a graceful cockerel which was perfect in every detail. This was to be the centre-piece of a buffet.

It has taken 12 people 48 hours to create the buffet, and in two hours it will be eaten.

Back in the restaurant the waiters, now looking elegant in their dinner jackets, were "laying up" with gleaming silver, shining glass, and stiff white tablecloths. From the dingy, ill-lit "caff" of early morning, was slowly emerging the Emperor Napoleon Banqueting Room.

I was allowed to help skin the salmon trout – a job that requires infinite patience. "Gently – very gently, Simon – use the whole blade of the knife!" One over-anxious jab and the whole fish disintegrates. "Careful now – you're not making a fish pie!"

The chandeliers were lit and the guests began to arrive. The air was humming with excitement and the Café Royal looked magnificent. The buffet table surmounted by Philip's gleaming ice sculpture was a poem of beautifully-arranged salmon trout, piped duchesse potatoes and a salad that was truly a work of art. It was a triumph!

Skinning a salmon trout needed a lot of patience. One false move and you've made a fish pie.

I felt as though I wanted to run out into the restaurant in my chef's hat, calling out "Stop – stop, you vandals," as the ruthless, gleaming spoons seared into our glorious creation.

"That's what it's for, Simon – for eating," said Roger. "And now, before you go, you can give us a hand with about 500 dirty pans."

The banquet was over. Now all I had to do was wash up 500 dirty pans.

At four o'clock in the afternoon, when the last pan was washed and preparations were well underway for dinner that night, I saw two porters lift the remains of Philip Ben's half-melted cockerel from its tray and fling it into a metal sink.

"All art's quite useless," Oscar Wilde said in the Café Royal, almost a hundred years ago.

ANIMALS IN DANGER

These animals are in danger.

Man is their enemy. For centuries he has killed tigers for their magnificent coats and rhinos for their ivory horns. He cuts down the forests which are home to the Orang Utan and pollutes the clean streams where the otter needs to swim. In a few years' time, hundreds of strange and beautiful creatures will walk the earth no more.

The DODO was a big, heavy bird, about as big as a swan, with a clumsy body and a huge head and beak. It had tiny wings, so it couldn't fly, and thick short legs, so it couldn't run fast. It had no way of escaping from its enemies.

Dead as the Dodo

1 In 1507 a band of Portuguese seamen on their way to the East Indies discovered an uncharted island in the Indian Ocean. When they went ashore they found the island so full of enormous birds they named it the Isle of Swans, because swans were the biggest birds they knew.

2   The men walked towards the birds who just stayed where they were, without moving. Some of them even walked *towards* the first men they had ever seen. They were so friendly and unafraid, the seamen gave them the name DODO – from the Portuguese word Doudo, which means stupid.

5   The hen dodo laid just one egg each year, so there were never many chicks growing up on the island.

3   In 1598 the island was taken over by the Dutch, who named it Mauritius. It was a useful port of call between Europe, Africa and Asia, and many ships weighed anchor there.

4   The seamen and their passengers all killed the dodos – for food, although they weren't very good to eat – or for sport, or to take back to Europe to show people. And still the dodos were friendly and didn't run away! Instead, the "Stupid Birds" stood and looked at their enemies. They ate seeds and wild plants and did no harm to anyone.

6   People in Europe were fascinated by the tales of the strange bird. And in 1683, at a fair in London, a booth displayed a painted Dodo on a cloth. Inside, a rather miserable Dodo was put on view to the curious crowds.

7 Scientists were interested, too, and skeletons and stuffed birds were brought back for them to study. They said the most amazing thing about the Dodo was that it was found on the Isle of Mauritius and nowhere else in the whole world. And they kept warning that if people went on killing dodos, they would soon become extinct. No one took any notice.

8 Back on Mauritius there were not nearly so many dodos now. Sailors not only killed them themselves – they had brought pigs to the island and they ate the eggs and young chicks. And still nobody paid any attention to the scientists' warning that the Dodo was an endangered species. The slaughter went on.

9 In 1681 a seaman fired – and killed the very last surviving dodo. Now there were no more alive, anywhere in the world.

10 The Dodo – the bird that was too stupid to run away from its enemies – had become extinct.

There's an expression – "As Dead As the Dodo" – and it is very useful to remember it, and to remember what happened to the Dodo.
When animal lovers today warn that endangered species may become extinct, they are told: "It could never happen!" But it *did* happen to the Dodo – and it could happen just as easily to the whale and the tiger and the otter, as well as hundreds more. And then they, too, would be "AS DEAD AS THE DODO".

THE CASE OF
THE SECRET ELEPHANTS

Can you solve this case?

Six careless mistakes gave away the crook.

We spotted them – can you?

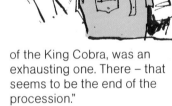

The sound of drumbeats echoed through the streets of Kandy – a thousand dancers leapt boisterously into the air, and in the middle of it all, stately, magnificent, and enormous, strode the elephants, wearing sumptuous costumes and moving with a massive, sacred dignity.

"I don't think I will ever get over Sri Lanka," remarked Bob.

His uncle, globe-trotting private detective – former Police Superintendent McCann, laughed.

"It's a great country," he agreed.

They were both standing at the side of the lake in Kandy, the largest town in the Sri Lankan hill country, watching one of the great religious festivals of the world – a mighty procession around the town with nearly one hundred elephants. Star of the great pageant of both Buddhist and Hindu religions was mighty Raja, the giant tusker that carried a replica of the Buddha's tooth on his back.

"It's wonderful to be here for the festival," Bob continued. "Especially since you were able to tell me so much about it. This is a great place for a holiday."

"I certainly need a holiday," said McCann. "The last case, over in India, with the Maharajah's diamond and the curious problem

of the King Cobra, was an exhausting one. There – that seems to be the end of the procession."

"You're right," Bob agreed. "Aren't elephants wonderful? The way they work, I mean."

"Amazing animals," said McCann. "Did you know African elephants are never used for work, but Indian elephants, like these, are still used all the time?"

"How strange," said Bob, gazing along the street. "I hear they're very keen on cricket here – any chance of getting to play a match, do you think?"

The last elephant in the great procession was now out of sight. Bob turned to his uncle, wanting to hear more about the diamond case, when a stout and dapper little man wearing a tan suit, a bow tie and a worried expression stopped in front of them, looking suddenly delighted and amazed.

"Oh, my goodness gracious me, you are the great detective McCann, I am thinking!"

McCann smiled at the agitated Sri Lankan. "That's me!"

"Mr McCann, you must help me. I am in terrible, terrible trouble!"

"Bang goes my holiday," McCann murmured ruefully. But Bob saw that his eyes were gleaming; there was nothing in the world McCann liked better than hunting criminals.

"What's the trouble, then?" he asked.

"My name is Kumarajaratnapura – please call me Kumar. I am the head of the government wildlife organisation, and I am being here in Kandy for the purposes of running an international conference on elephants. There is a big problem with people shooting the poor beasts for their tusks, which they sell for the ivory."

"It's very valuable stuff," Bob put in.

"Indeed, indeed – they make plenty, plenty money and we must worry. These people kill elephants – one day comes when there are no more elephants – all dead. Very bad thing, isn't it? Number of wild elephants gets smaller every year."

"Kandy is full of elephants," protested Bob.

"Yes, yes, yes – the working elephant is very important – we use them all the time – much better than tractor. But the wild elephants I am talking about, they are in trouble.

"And a terrible thing has happened. I have an office here at headquarters in Kandy – an office I always keep locked; no one ever goes in there. On that desk is a top secret report. I am telling you, in strictest confidence Mr McCann, sir, the report is about the secret elephant sanctuary of Dama. Not even the elephant experts at the conference know about Dama.

"This is not for tourists, I am telling you. It is for science and for conservation; and many hundreds of wild elephants are living in Dama.

"No bad men with rifles ever trouble them. Very, very fine indeed."

"But I am telling you left and right, Mr McCann, someone has broken the lock of my office and stolen this report. Now the bad persons know where the elephants are living, so he goes with gun and shoots them all and surely sells their tusks for millions of rupees." Kumar's chubby face crumpled, and his eyes filled with tears at the thought.

"Kumar," said McCann. "I'd like to come with you to headquarters. This is bad trouble."

The trio walked briskly through the dusty, crowded streets thronged with sari-clad ladies, men in long white skirts, smoking huge cigars, and the occasional stately elephant ridden skilfully by his rider or mahout.

Headquarters was a large, airy building. Entering through a gate, the new arrivals found themselves in a courtyard, in which a small number of men were standing in groups, talking. Kumar introduced McCann and Bob.

"Holy smoke, Mr McCann, what brings a guy like you here?" trumpeted a tall and scrawny American wearing a baseball cap.

First reactions always interested McCann, Bob knew, and he kept his ears pricked and his eyes open, hoping to catch one of these men in a flash of guilt.

McCann replied to the American vaguely: "Just passing by."

"You are in the elephants interested, ja?" asked a sweating, serious-looking man named Doctor Schwarzkopf.

"A little," said McCann. "You're a long way from Germany, Doctor."

Schwarzkopf laughed. "I have never been to Germany! I am from Switzerland coming. I spend all my travelling time in India and Sri Lanka studying the elephants."

McCann smiled, and asked the doctor: "What's this pretty little toy?" McCann indicated a stout, silver stick with a hook at one end, which leant against the wall of the courtyard close by where Bob was standing.

Kumar answered for the Swiss: "This is being an elephant goad, used by mahout for controlling elephant."

"Frightfully useful thing, don't you know?" remarked an Englishman named Professor Moreland, who was wearing beautifully tailored white trousers and a loose-fitting salmon-coloured silk shirt.

"I'm sure," said McCann, turning to the elegant professor, "you have a lot of interest in elephants yourself, I imagine."

"Oh yes, absolutely. Studied 'em for years. Remarkable animals, amazing. And numbers of wild elephants are rising steadily these days, if you know what I mean. Frightfully good news."

"Is this your first time in Sri Lanka?" asked McCann.

"Been here simply billions of times.

I always try to get out for the great Muslim festival that was held today. It's a splendid spot, frightfully good chaps and all that sort of rot. But to tell you the truth, I know Africa better. I've been studying their working elephants for years."

"What do you think about Sri Lanka's work for wild elephants?"

"I think it's all absolutely marvellous, quite frankly. I'm really impressed by the way these chaps have got their things all sorted out. This sanctuary at Dama, for instance – absolutely brilliant, to my way of thinking. I mean, isn't it?"

"Nobody could deny that," said McCann. Bob chipped in: "Why do you like elephants so much, Professor Moreland?"

Kumar, standing beside McCann, took a deep breath, plainly wanting to say his piece on how much he loved elephants himself. But McCann halted him with a hand on his shoulder.

"Hard to say," the nattily dressed professor said. "But the animals are simply the most frightfully beautiful things. I mean, aren't they? Look, for example, at the wonderful photograph of elephants you have on the wall of your office here, Mr Kumar."

"Yes, indeed, professor," said Kumar. "You are absolutely right, my friend. However, duty is now calling us: the conference must continue. The good doctor of Germany, whose name I am unable to say, is to be speaking to us on the problems of keeping the elephants in captivity. We must be working, my good sir."

Moreland gave them all a charming smile. "Well, as a matter of fact, sorry to seem so frightfully lazy and all that, but I heard old Schwarzkopf's talk before, in Bonn. I'll give it a miss and stroll down to the lake and see you all back for lunch, if that's all right with everyone."

McCann then did a very extraordinary thing. He leant forward, and with his open palm, slapped the elegant professor in the stomach. You would have expected a dull sound of flesh against flesh: instead, there was a loud smacking noise, as if McCann had struck a pile of paper.

Moreland's reactions were equally extraordinary. He snarled, removing every trace of phoney charm from his face, bowled hapless Kumar off his feet and sprinted for the gate.

Bob was first to move. He seized the silver elephant goad that stood near him and hurled it low and hard, spinning wildly. It was a first-class throw – the throw of a brilliant cricketer. And Bob certainly hit the wicket.

The catherine-wheeling stick spun into the sprinting legs of the fleeing Moreland: the man went down like a shot elephant. In a flash, McCann had him by the scruff of the neck. With his free hand, he ripped the elegant salmon shirt from the professor's cringing body: tucked in the waistband of his exquisite trousers was a report. It was marked: "TOP SECRET : Report on Elephant Sanctuary at Dama."

"Oh, my gracious golly," said Kumar, dusting himself down after his tumble, his eyes wide with astonishment. "This is a most extraordinary thing, I am thinking."

"Yes," said McCann. "The man Moreland stole your report. He was undoubtedly in the pay of a gang of elephant-shooting, ivory-selling, international bandits. He is not really a professor at all."

"But how are you knowing this thing?"

"Bob," McCann grinned. "You know my methods. How did I know?"

"My feeling is that the phoney professor made six mistakes, all of them very foolish."

Kumar gasped. "This is witchcraft!"

"No," said McCann. "Just detective work." He looked modestly down at his boots.

It was left to Bob to sum up. "Thanks to my uncle," he said, "the elephants of Sri Lanka will be able to sleep easier in their vast and secret reservation."

Did you spot the six mistakes? Check your answers on page 76.

Now Find a Mirror!

SOLUTIONS

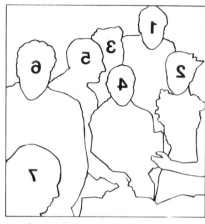

1 Robert Moreton 2 Julie Andrews
3 Hattie Jacques 4 Archie Andrews
5 Peter Brough 6 Max Bygraves
7 Roy Speer

The Case of the Secret Elephants

1 Moreland said that the wild elephant population was rising. A real elephant expert, like Kumar, would know that the opposite is true. Kumar had, in fact, told McCann that the wild population was actually falling.

2 Moreland, who claimed to have been in Sri Lanka often, said that the procession was a Muslim festival. McCann had already told Bob it is, in fact, Buddhist and Hindu. Someone who had really been often in Sri Lanka would know this.

3 Moreland claimed to have studied working elephants in Africa. But as McCann told Bob, there are no working elephants in Africa. Plainly, Moreland could not be an elephant expert as he claimed.

4 Moreland knew about the secret sanctuary at Dama. Kumar said no one at the conference knew about Dama: this means Moreland must have stolen the report.

5 Kumar said no one ever went into his office – it was always kept locked. But Moreland talked about a picture on the wall. The only way he could have seen the picture was when he stole the report.

6 Moreland claimed to have heard Schwarzkopf's talk in Bonn, which is in Germany. But Schwarzkopf had already told McCann that he had never been to Germany. Moreland was caught out in a lie that showed his ignorance of top elephant experts. Obviously he could not be an expert himself, as he claimed.

Puzzle Pictures

1 Keeping fit with Belly Dancer Tina Hobin.

2 Roy Castle created a World Tap Dancing Record in 1979. 3½ years later, Julie Parker, one of the 522 dancers who took part, landed a leading West End role in The Sound of Music.

3 Building our greenhouse in the Blue Peter garden, helped by Percy Thrower.

4 The Royal Navy's Window Ladder Display Team from HMS Excellent.

5 The first of the Blue Peter Bungalows for the Disabled was opened by our friend, Joey Deacon, in October 1981. Very sadly, Joey, who had inspired our Great Blue Peter Bring and Buy Sale for the Disabled Appeal, died two months later.

6 This papier-mâché Sarah is the work of sculptor, Terry Wall.

7 With inside legs of 5½ metres and trouser bottoms measuring 1 metre across, this inflatable is the largest pair of jeans in the world.

8 Escapologist Howard Peters took 45 seconds to get out of the 33 metre length of rope we'd tied him up in.

9 Mrs Edith Cooper of New Milton and her vintage washing machine. Bought in 1939 for £34, it's still going strong and can steam puddings as well as wash clothes.

10 A Baked Bean Eat In was held by the 28th Oxford (Littlemore) Cub Scout Pack to celebrate the 75th Anniversary of the Scouting Movement.

ACKNOWLEDGEMENTS

Co-ordinator: **Gillian Farnsworth**.

Designed by: **David Playne**, assisted by Nick Allen, Simon Borrough, Richard Brown, Jon Davis, Jacquie Govier, Nicholas Rous and Lois Wigens.

Seeing Double, *Dead as the Dodo*, and *The Honourable Pilot* were written by **Dorothy Smith**.

Puppet on a String, *Rudolph the Red-nosed Reindeer* and *Apple Cake* by **Margaret Parnell**. The Case of the Secret Elephants was written by **Simon Barnes**.

Japan was written by **Renny Rye**.

Dead as the Dodo was illustrated by **Robert Broomfield**.

All photographs were taken by Joan Williams, David Clarke, Michael Cullen, Philip Carr, John Jefford, Peter Lane, Ian Oliver, Renny Rye, Nick Allen, Alex Doble, David Playne, Kenneth Smith and Terry Odem with the exception of:

Jin Li & Yehudi Menuhin (p.9) by permission of EMI; Meldog (p.20) by Ian Wright/Sunday Times; Ar4 (p.20) by Paul Duncan Associates; Transglobe picture (p.22) by David Mason; Skidoo, Penguins & Bothy jumping (p.23) by Bryn Campbell/Observer Magazine; Ginny on phone and Bothy alone (p.23) by Sir Ranulph Fiennes; c/u face (p.23) by Syndication International; Corset boxes & copper torsos (p.25) and Amori belt & Freda Cox (p.26) by Leicestershire Museums, Art Galleries & Record Services; Shogun Ieyasu (p.36) by International Society for Educational Information, Tokyo. Morph animated, Morph with title, and David Sproxton & Peter Lord (pp. 38–40) were taken by David Sproxton & Peter Lord; Refectory and Cloisters (p.46) by J. Allan Cash; Oldest figure & Frank Travis (p.48) and B/w group (p.49) by permission of Valentine Vox; Endurance photographs (pp.50–53) by Robin Mudge; *Mary Rose* (p.59) by Historical Reproductions Ltd. C/o *Mary Rose* Trust; Diver (p.60) and underwater picture (p.61) by *Mary Rose* Trust. Oscar Wilde & Marie Lloyd (p.66) by BBC Hulton Picture Library; Otter & Tiger (p.69) by Bruce Coleman Ltd., Rhinoceros (p.69) by Heather Angel; Elephant & Orang Utan (p.69) by World Wildlife Fund; Panda (p.69) by Zoological Society of London.

USEFUL INFORMATION

British Sub Aqua Club
16 Upper Woburn Place, London WC1 HOQR

Japanese Information Office
9 Grosvenor Square, London W.1.

St Michael's Mount
Manor Office, Marazion, Cornwall.

Mont St Michel
Caen, Normandy, France.

The Symington Collection
Leicestershire Museum, Leicester.

Foundations of Fashion Corsetry from 1856 to the Present Day
by Christopher Page, published by Leicestershire Museum price £3.50.

"I Can See Your Lips Moving"
The history and art of ventriloquism by Valentine Vox, published by Kaye & Ward, price £12.50.

OXFAM
Campaign Manager, 274 Banbury Road, Oxford, OX2 7DZ

Roadline UK Ltd.
The Merton Centre, 45 St. Peter's Street, Bedford, MK40 8UB

Phillips
7 Blenheim Street, New Bond Street, London W.1.

The Mary Rose Trust
The Old Bond Store, Warblington Street, Portsmouth.

Transglobe Expedition
Westlink House, 981 Great West Road, Brentford, Middlesex. TW8 9DN

Hearing Dogs for the Deaf
Royal National Institute for the Deaf, 105 Gower Street, London WC1E 6AH

Guide Dogs for the Blind Association
Alexandra House, 7–11 Park Street, Windsor, Berkshire.

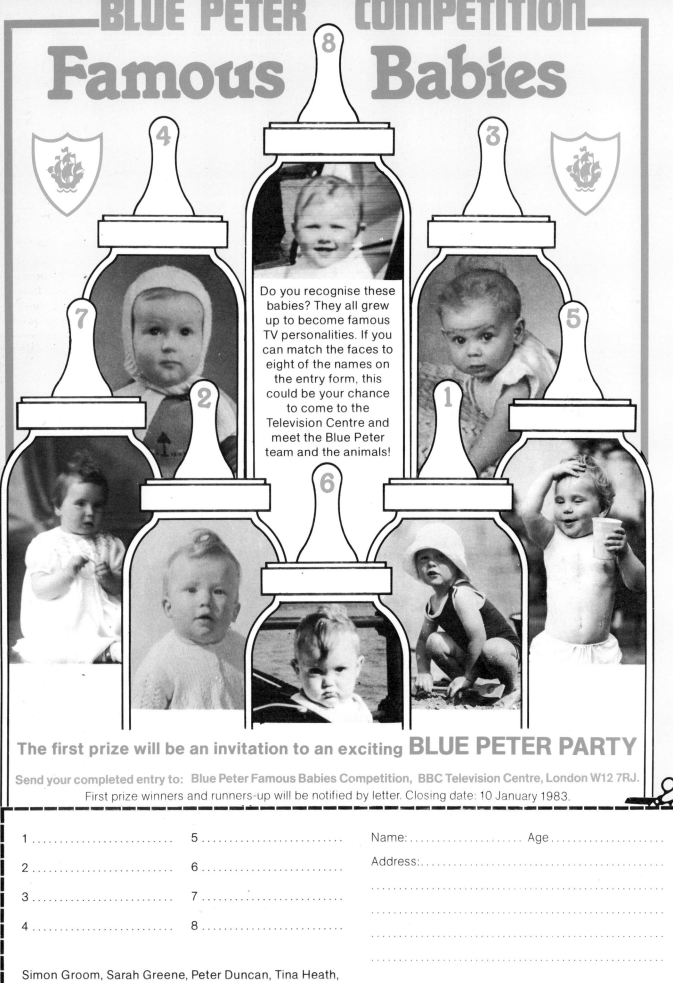

BLUE PETER COMPETITION
Famous Babies

Do you recognise these babies? They all grew up to become famous TV personalities. If you can match the faces to eight of the names on the entry form, this could be your chance to come to the Television Centre and meet the Blue Peter team and the animals!

The first prize will be an invitation to an exciting BLUE PETER PARTY

Send your completed entry to: Blue Peter Famous Babies Competition, BBC Television Centre, London W12 7RJ.
First prize winners and runners-up will be notified by letter. Closing date: 10 January 1983.

1 ....
2 ....
3 ....
4 ....

5 ....
6 ....
7 ....
8 ....

Name:.................... Age.....................
Address:...
....
....
....

Simon Groom, Sarah Greene, Peter Duncan, Tina Heath,
John Craven, Ruch Madoc, Keith Chegwin, Tony Hart, Brian Cant, Johnny Ball, Roy Castle, Johnny Morris.